"*Toughest People to Love* will make you a better leader, pastor, parent, and friend. But more than anything else, this book will guide you down a path of personal renewal and give you a new trajectory in your own journey to wholeness and integration. This is a book to read again and again as we seek to love the beautiful and broken people in our lives, including the person we see when we look in the mirror."

— FRED HARRELL
senior pastor of City Church
San Francisco

"This wise and winsome book on leadership takes us on a journey into the challenges and complexities of difficult relationships — with others and with ourselves. Reflecting the Christian wisdom that suffering can lead to human flourishing, DeGroat points us to the rest beyond bodily rest found paradoxically in the solitude and the deepening community with others that together center us in God."

— ERIC JOHNSON
director of the Society
for Christian Psychology

"Chuck DeGroat clearly understands the realities of pastoral ministry. This book is both theologically robust and practical and therefore takes a well-rounded approach to human formation. It will substantially help those who want to understand what Christian leadership, counseling, and friendship really mean."

— TYLER JOHNSON
lead pastor of
Redemption Gateway Church,
Mesa, Arizona

toughest people to love

how to understand, lead, and love
the difficult people in your life —
including yourself

Chuck DeGroat

William B. Eerdmans Publishing Company
Grand Rapids, Michigan / Cambridge, U.K.

Published 2014 by

Wm. B. Eerdmans Publishing Co.

2140 Oak Industrial Drive N.E., Grand Rapids, Michigan 49505 /
P.O. Box 163, Cambridge CB3 9PU U.K.

Printed in the United States of America

20 19 18 17 16 15 14   7 6 5 4 3 2 1

Library of Congress Cataloging-in-Publication Data

DeGroat, Chuck.
Toughest people to love: how to understand, lead, and love the
difficult people in your life — including yourself / Chuck DeGroat.
pages   cm
Includes bibliographical references.
ISBN 978-0-8028-7143-5 (pbk.: alk. paper)
1. Conflict management — Religious aspects — Christianity.
2. Interpersonal conflict — Religious aspects — Christianity.
3. Interpersonal relations — Religious aspects — Christianity.
4. Love — Religious aspects — Christianity.   I. Title.

BV4597.53.C58D44   2014
248.4 — dc23

2014002440

www.eerdmans.com

Contents

Introduction

I am the true vine, and my Father is the gardener.

JOHN 15:1

We keep bringing in mechanics when what we need
are gardeners.

PETER SENGE

You're blessed when you get your inside world —
your mind and heart — put right. Then you can see God
in the outside world.

MATTHEW 5:8 *(THE MESSAGE)*

O RGANIZATIONAL GURU PETER SENGE wrote one of the
best articles on leadership I have ever read. People who know
me are aware that I'm generally suspicious of so-called "leadership
experts." But Senge proposed what seemed like a Copernican revo-
lution in leadership, one that toppled the unquestioned principles
of management and organizations. He argued that organizations
are, in fact, *organisms* — living things — like gardens. Challenging
modernist leadership assumptions that promote rigid, hierarchical,
and mechanistic work environments, Senge envisioned a relational
and soulful approach to leading people, one that struck me as wise
and much needed.

Senge also challenged the sacred authority of the CEO, the
unquestioned and invulnerable leader who leads by control and

compliance. He advocated for a new kind of leader: one who is relational, vulnerable, humble, willing to learn (and even fail); one who leads by integrity rather than manipulation. Since I was a young leader myself, Senge's words struck me to the core:

> Deep change comes only through real personal growth — through learning and unlearning. This is the kind of generative work that most executives are precluded from doing by the mechanical mind-set and by the cult of the hero-leader: The hero-leader is the one with "the answers." Most of the other people in the organization can't make deep changes, because they're operating out of compliance, rather than out of commitment. Commitment comes about only when people determine that you are asking them to do something that they really care about. For that reason, if you create compliance-oriented change, you'll get change — but you'll preclude the deeper processes that lead to commitment, and you'll prevent the emergence of self-generated change. Again, you end up creating a kind of addiction: People change as long as they're being commanded to change — or as long as they can be forced to change. But, as a result, they become still more dependent on change that's driven from the top.[1]

As a recent seminary graduate and a new pastor, I felt as if I'd received a vision for pastoral ministry that had never been articulated in seminary or through my internship process. In my work in a small business and then during my years of seminary studies, I had observed many leaders. Most of them were very strong, but they seemed insecure. They thought it was important to lead from a posture of command and control, but they seemed deeply afraid to be questioned or to fail.

Senge says, "We keep bringing in mechanics when what we need are gardeners." As I read his words, it struck me that Jesus had similar things to say. Critiquing the rigid, hierarchical Pharisaism of his day, Jesus turned leadership upside-down — empowering the seemingly incapable, telling stories of vineyards and fields and sheep that needed the self-sacrificial tending of the soul-gardeners. Jesus, in other words, was not a command-and-control leader but a gardener of souls.

Now, let's face it — command and control works, at least for a time. It gives leaders that all-too-illusive sense of control, particularly when they feel they're in over their head. Most of us, I suspect, don't want to be leadership bullies. We'd prefer not to lead with an iron fist. But when we feel the inevitable internal chaos that comes with leading people, we default to what seems to work. Most of us are not skilled in the art of leading broken and wounded souls.

Perhaps you picked up this book because you were having a difficult time of leadership yourself, hoping it might give you a bit more control amid the chaos. Perhaps you (like me) crave the ultimate handbook for understanding and "fixing" people.

This is not that book. Instead, I'm offering a bigger vision for human relating, one that might even allow you to relinquish the need for control. Eugene Peterson's wonderful memoir, *Pastor*, reminds us that we're called to be contemplative, not competitive.[2] People are not problems to be fixed, Peterson suggests, but image-bearers to be known. As contemplatives, we turn our focus to seeing God in the ordinary moments, in the broken lives of people, and in our own humanness. We lead from a posture of self-sacrificial love — the deep secret of God's kingdom — instead of from a posture of competition, control, and manipulation.

If the soul is a garden to be tended to, as all of God's good creation is, then we must approach the garden with a sense of sacred awe. People are profoundly complex: both beautiful and broken, productive and paralyzed, fruitful and foolish. In my work over the past fifteen years as a pastor, a seminary professor, a therapist, and a church leader, I've been tempted in my worst moments to see only the problems and failures. Surveying the broken body of Christ, I sometimes opt for the quick and easy cosmetic change rather than the hard work of soul gardening. Too often, I've abandoned sacred awe for cynicism, self-protection, and fearful reactivity. The best leaders I've talked to admit the same.

In this book I will address the dark side of people. But I'm convinced that in God's economy of grace, nothing is wasted — not our failures, not even our big sins. In our darkest hour, the Father sees us and runs wildly toward us, arms open in joyful compassion (Luke 15:20). He doesn't fear our sinful chaos. Rather, the great Gardener sees an opportunity to cultivate us, to grow us, to renew us. Jesus transforms our little deaths of failure and sin into redemptive opportunities for growth and renewal. As Jesus says, "Very truly I tell you, unless a kernel of wheat falls to the ground and dies, it remains only a single seed. But if it dies, it produces many seeds" (John 12:24). Our failures are often opportunities for new beginnings.

The Best Leaders: Wounded Healers

One day I decided to Google my name to see what was being said about me in cyberspace. While I was clicking through various blogs and Web sites, it dawned on me that none of them included references to my painful failures and disappointments. Of course, that wasn't what I had Googled my name to see. But the real truth about me cannot be found on Web sites and blogs, not even those I write myself. Who I am today is a composite of many things, from my DNA to the various people in my life to my struggles and failures.

I've made it a bit of a hobby to study the stories of great Christian leaders, with a special focus on the painful struggles in their lives. I think of St. Augustine, who rehearsed his life of sexual addiction in his famous *Confessions*. Or St. Teresa of Ávila, who experienced years of prolonged spiritual dryness. Or Charles Spurgeon, who battled such severe depression that he was frequently unable to preach. Or Catherine of Siena, whose chronic illness was no small factor in her becoming a rare female Christian leader in fourteenth-century Italy. These people remind me to consider my own story, my own difficulty, before presuming to engage the struggles of others.

Perhaps that's why I was so drawn to *Lincoln's Melancholy*, a biography of Abraham Lincoln by Joshua Shenk. The fact that Lincoln was depressed and at times even suicidal is widely known, but I found myself gripped by the particulars of his story: failure, a broken relationship, an imperfect pedigree, a genetic burden. And yet Lincoln's own woundedness, the author argues, brought healing to a nation.

When I read Henri Nouwen's *The Wounded Healer* as a young seminary student, I wondered why a seminary professor would want us dwelling on the morbid and unhelpful topic of our own pain. Surely I had better things to do: study Greek, learn how to preach, master biblical exegesis. Little did I know that my own brokenness would be the conduit of much more healing in the long run.

I hope this book is a product of hard lessons learned. I pray that we'll all be compelled to love others, not as those who've been to the mountaintop and are "experts" and "mechanics" — command-and-control leaders — but as leaders who know our own brokenness and who have found a greater wellspring in God's deeper love.

A Road Map

So, what will we explore in this book?

In Part 1, we'll explore the basics of how people work. The first chapter, "A Vision for Those We Lead, a Vision for Ourselves," sets the tone for the rest of the book. You'll notice that I won't let you off the hook if you're someone who is in charge. In fact, I'm convinced that leaders are called to examine ourselves very carefully as we attempt to figure out others. Don't read on if you're not ready for what you'll find when you turn the microscope on yourself!

Chapter 2 is entitled "Understanding Our Story." This is psychology for the layperson, and we'll learn that there's much more to human beings than meets the eye. (Every good leader I've ever met is a closet psychologist. In fact, many leaders thrive on understanding what makes people tick.) It's always humbling when we recognize what is happening beneath the surface of a difficult person.

In Part 2 we'll explore the theme of leading and loving difficult people. We begin in Chapter 3 with a basic introduction to personality disorders. Have you ever dealt with a narcissist? How should you handle the drama addict in your church? We'll explore the more common disorders with an eye toward helping others while maintaining some sense of sanity ourselves.

Chapter 4 is titled "Addictions: Loving in the Dark." Rarely have I found pastors and leaders more confounded than when they're dealing with addicts. There is a twist in this chapter — a new way of thinking about addiction that I believe will revolutionize the way you approach the addict's despair.

Chapter 5 presents a model for dealing with the most difficult people you'll face. I call it "Loving the Fool: When Relationships Turn Ugly." In it we'll summarize everything we've learned thus far in three major categories that reveal the heart of a type of person the Bible calls the "fool."

Part 3 assumes that the best help we can give another person is to deal with ourselves. And so I invite you on that journey.

In Chapter 6 I share my own story in a chapter I've titled "Growing through Pain: The Gift of the Dark." We'll discuss the ancient idea of "the dark night of the soul" by looking at one of my own dark nights. We often wonder whether God can do anything with our own darkness, and the good news is that God can.

Chapter 7 is called "Living with Wholeness: Rest and Resiliency in the Leader's Life." Wholeness, I believe, is a deeply biblical concept. It has been wrongfully relegated to the category of pop psychology, so I use the great nineteenth-century preacher Charles Spurgeon to help revive it. If you've ever been challenged to "keep the Sabbath," prepare to have your categories blown apart. If you're exhausted, prepare for some refreshment.

Finally, we end with a chapter titled "Growing into Leadership Maturity: Self-Care and the Art of Shadow-Boxing." It is vitally important that leaders care for themselves. But take note: self-care includes honest self-assessment. I borrow the term "shadow-boxing" from a favorite writer of mine to talk about a way of exploring our own lives for the sake of leading others.

Part 1

UNDERSTANDING PEOPLE

a vision for those we lead, a vision for ourselves

Leadership is not about problems and decisions; it is a
profoundly relational enterprise that seeks to motivate
people toward a vision that will require significant change
and risk on everyone's part.

DAN ALLENDER

Ministers run the awful risk . . . of ceasing to be witnesses to
the presence [of a living God] in their own lives — let alone
in the lives of the people they are trying to minister to.

FREDERICK BUECHNER

It is always easier for us to want to purify other people,
and attempt a moral reformation among our neighbors.
(Yet) how much have I helped to make her what she is?

CHARLES SPURGEON

We are guides into God's most sublime secrets,
not security guards posted to protect them.

1 CORINTHIANS 4:1-2 *(THE MESSAGE)*

THE E-MAIL THE PASTOR received was riddled with accusations. He sat at his desk, battling a range of emotions: anger, disappointment, but mostly despair.

He'd never felt this low. His mind flashed back to a seminary class he had taken. He and his buddies sat in the back row, laughing at stories the professor told about depressed pastors. He thought of his best friend, a successful church planter who never seemed to fail at anything. He recalled that his wife had urged him to get therapy three years ago. He thought of the sermon he had no motivation to finish. And for the first time he thought, *Maybe I'm not cut out for this.*

It'd Be Easier without People

Statistics show that 80 percent of new pastors leave the ministry within five years. A friend once remarked, "If they were able to pastor churches without people, they might last ten years." Most pastors that researchers survey feel overworked, stressed, inadequately prepared for the complexities of ministry, and subject to the unrealistically high expectations of their parishioners.[1] My own research with pastors who had spent five years in ministry revealed one menace that affected them more than any other: difficult people.[2] In my research interviews, many pastors lamented that the seminary they had attended provided little or no training in dealing with difficult people. They also admitted that they might not have entered the ministry if they had known how complex it would be.

Burnout, compassion fatigue, anxiety, depression, addiction, self-doubt — in most leaders I know, these problems can be traced to relational difficulties of some kind.

My peers in the corporate world report similar findings. As a therapist, I've counseled many leaders in business, politics, church, education, and more. A client of mine in the chaotic tech industry, overwhelmed by dysfunctional behavior of his bosses and those he supervised, said, "I love my machines, and they love me. But I hate people, and I think they're beginning to notice."

Can you relate? Do you sometimes wonder if life might be easier without your complicated employees or your demanding congregation or your difficult leaders?

And then, to complicate the picture, there is *you*. Most of us can get away from others for a while, but we can't get away from ourselves. Truth be told, we're part of the problem. It's easy to complain about the failures and inadequacies of those around us, but in the dark corners of our soul lie hidden our own eccentricities, deficiencies, and inadequacies. Between the "problem people" we deal with and our own inadequacies, it often seems impossible to find a way through the mess of human dysfunction. This situation slowly chips away at our idealism about what leadership should be like.

After spending two years in a Master of Divinity program, a series of difficult experiences in my own life led me to pursue a Master of Arts in Counseling degree. That first semester in the counseling clinic, I listened to the stories of men and women who'd experienced abuse, betrayal, and addiction; the stories of couples on the brink of divorce; and the stories of kids grieving the chaos in their families. My idealism about pastoral ministry began to dissipate. I had gone to seminary imagining that someday I'd find myself in a large office, surrounded by books, speaking each Sunday to an eager group of "followers" who'd take notes on my brilliant sermons. So much for that!

My view of people was rationalistic and mechanistic: I'd deliver the sermon; they would listen; the church would thrive. I'd provide solid theological information and some tried-and-true behavioral directives, and people would grow. What I learned during that critical two-year counseling program was that to lead people we've got to help them discover *a vision for themselves.* God didn't create human beings to operate like machines; to many of us, that is a truly remarkable revelation. To be human, instead, is to be in relation with God and with others. Being human is complex, messy, and much harder than we ever imagine it will be.

The Need for Vision

Slowly I began to see people not as machines to be fixed but as image-bearing humans who needed tending. One of the "aha" moments of discovery occurred early in my ministry career when a friend offered some sage advice. I had hit a rut in my pastoral life, fatigued by the complicated people I was trying to help. Most disheartening to me was the narcissistic executive who would "power up" in our pastoral counseling sessions, firing accusations at his wife like a lawyer nailing a case, and even intimidating me whenever he saw a chink in my pastoral armor.

"Chuck, you're young," he once said with a condescending smile. "You've only been married a short time. You probably don't understand what it's like to endure a woman's crazy mood swings." He was a master intimidator, and I wasn't sure how to handle the situation. Part of me just wanted out.

In a meeting with fellow counseling interns, I told my sad tale, looking both for sympathy and for a way out of this pastoral-care mess. And then my friend said something life-changing — something so truthful and profound that I felt as if she'd broken into the darkness of my cave of perception.

"You know, he has a story too."

My first thought was, *Umm, what about me? I'm the victim here. How about some pity for the poor therapist of this jerk?* But I swallowed those immediate feelings and asked what she meant.

"He has a story," she said. "Aren't you just a bit curious about it?" With one question, she rehumanized the man. Compassion welled up in my soul as I began to wonder about his life's story. Had he been bullied at some point? Had he, perhaps, been a victim of abuse? And how powerless must he feel inside to so aggressively overpower the people he loved the most?

Our default mode when we deal with difficult people is to demand repentance or to devise fix-it strategies or to offer insights to straighten people out. But working with people requires a special kind of vision. It requires us to see the bigger picture. Whether we're working with one difficult individual or with an entire congregation or company, our challenge is to keep that larger perspective in mind.

Visionary leadership is not reactive. It refuses to arrogantly offer the right solution or give the right answer. Rather, leading with vision requires that we *relate* to people. Dan Allender writes,

> Leadership is not about problems and decisions; it is a profoundly relational enterprise that seeks to motivate people toward a vision that will require significant change and risk on everyone's part. Decisions are simply the doors that leaders, as well as followers, walk through to get to the land where redemption can be found.[3]

Leadership hinges on relationship, and that requires us to risk. And though I'm convinced that visionary, relational leadership is a bedrock Christian posture, we all have a disturbing bent toward relational immaturity. I see how easily I become cynical, dismissive, judgmental, and reactive. I see how quickly I'm tempted to blast back at the person who sends a critical e-mail, or judge the person who doesn't make progress fast enough, or get impatient with those I manage who don't accomplish exactly what I think they should.

Our journey toward dealing compassionately with difficult people doesn't simply require us to learn a bit more about others. It also requires us to become better acquainted with ourselves.

A Vision for Ourselves

Nineteenth-century urban preacher Charles Spurgeon once said, "It is always easier for us to want to purify other people, and attempt a moral reformation among our neighbors." But he immediately followed that observation with this: "(Yet) how much have I helped to make her what she is? If she is degenerate, how far is that degeneracy a result of my having fallen from the high standing which I ought to have occupied?"[4]

Spurgeon means that people are a complicated mess, and humility is our best medicine. While an arrogantly self-assured Donald Trump commands ratings for dramatically firing people on TV, the leaders who truly gain our respect — leaders like Desmond Tutu, Mother Teresa, Nelson Mandela, and Abraham Lincoln — show a remarkable capacity for both strength and humility.

This humble strength requires leaders to move toward a more mature self-understanding, but doing so confronts us with the greatest challenge of our lives. While it's surprisingly easy to grouse about difficult people we work with and manage, it's much harder for us to admit our own part in the dysfunction. We cannot lead well if we do not thoroughly understand our own motivations, inadequacies, and fears.

Some time ago I counseled someone who had received a series of negative reviews from his supervisor. The chief complaint was that this man did not relate and work well with his female coworkers. In our conversation it seemed that he was angling for some validation, hoping I'd agree with him that the women were the problem, not him.

In our hour together, I took some time to ask about his family upbringing and about his relationships with his mom, his sisters, and the women he'd dated. I was probing a bit, to be sure, but a kind of holy curiosity is necessary in counselors. We don't merely offer solutions; instead, we ask significant questions.

I discovered that the man was the youngest of four siblings, all girls except for him. Because he was frequently teased and often felt left out, he grew up secretly resentful of the females in his life and was quite unable to understand the feelings of fear and insecurity that would arise when he was around women.

As we talked, his eyes began to open. For the first time he began to examine his own life and his own story, identifying important themes from his past that continued in his present. Tears welled up for a childhood marked by loneliness, fear, and hidden anger. But then something remarkable happened. While it might have sufficed for him to explore his own pain, he instead began to grieve for the women in his life — girlfriends, classmates, coworkers — who had often been the victims of his reactivity and condescension.

In a short hour, this man began to understand himself in a way he never had before. And while the journey to self-understanding was just beginning, he was well on his way to greater maturity in all his relationships.

As leaders, we need to understand others. But we also need to recognize our own blind spots. If we don't, we inflict on others our unresolved issues and dysfunctions, doing great harm to those we lead.

I think often of the providence of an early encounter with a therapist who told me that without counseling I'd be a dangerous pastor. My immediate reaction was defensive, but in my own therapy, the depth and breadth of my blind spots have been revealed time and again. I've needed some prodding along the way, of course. Frederick Buechner, the Presbyterian pastor and writer, has been instrumental in my own journey. Many years ago his wise words gently prodded me toward self-understanding during a time when I was struggling with exhaustion and anger, and when family and friends were feeling the brunt of it. Buechner writes,

> Ministers run the awful risk . . . of ceasing to be witnesses to the presence in their own lives — let alone in the lives of the people they are trying to minister to — of a living God who transcends everything they think they know and can say about him and is full of extraordinary surprises. Instead they tend to become professionals who have mastered all the techniques of institutional religion and who speak on religious matters with what often seems a maximum of authority and a minimum of vital personal involvement. Their sermons often sound as bland as they sound bloodless. The faith they proclaim appears to be no longer rooted in or nourished by or challenged by their own lives but instead free-floating, secondhand, passionless. They sound, in other words, burnt out.[5]

Buechner continually diagnoses my own tendency to live without vision, to be oblivious to my own fears and insecurities. But he also reminds me that when I live that way, I can become a dangerous leader, one who operates with great control and certainty but with little vulnerability and self-awareness.

Interestingly, secular management experts are recognizing more and more that honest self-awareness is the backbone of healthy leadership. In the Arbinger Institute's best-selling book *Leadership and Self-Deception*, the authors write,

> Self-deception . . . blinds us to the true causes of problems, and once we're blind, all the "solutions" we can think of will actually make matters worse. Whether at work or at home, self-deception obscures the truth about ourselves, corrupts our view of others and our circumstances, and inhibits our ability to make wise and helpful decisions. To the extent that

we are self-deceived, our happiness and our leadership [are] compromised at every turn.[6]

Self-awareness, in turn, leads to greater transparency — a cornerstone of effective leadership.[7] Whenever I teach pastors and leaders, this is a great surprise to them. We are conditioned to believe that self-awareness and transparency are by-products of weak leadership. The principles of "developing a thick skin," of "keeping your friends close and your enemies closer," and "keeping your cards close to your vest" seem to represent long-accepted wisdom about successful leadership. But the very best insights of secular leaders today reveal a much different truth. The most effective leaders demonstrate integrity, lead transparently, and cultivate trust.

So the challenge is this: We must gain a greater vision of our own lives, marked by honest self-understanding and a clear sense of how the significant themes of our stories will replay in the present.[8] As we'll see in the coming pages, looking at our own lives is integral to leading and loving others well.

Relational to Our Core

We're living in a revolutionary time. The modernist belief in control and precision is fading as both the universe and human beings are shown to be more complex than we ever imagined. Perhaps we're rediscovering the wisdom of the book of Job, where the apparently "right" answers don't touch the real pain or effect real change (see Job 6), frustrating those of us who've committed our lives to impacting others.

Today's neuroscientists are rediscovering what attachment psychologists recognized thirty years ago, what the writer of Genesis penned in the first pages of Scripture, and what Christian mystics knew in ancient times: we are, at our core, *relational* beings. This is a frightening reality for those who prefer a more rational, mechanical, and behavioral model. We're discovering that from birth to death our brain thrives or withers based on the health of our relationships. And we're discovering that, as Curt Thompson puts it, "the process of reflecting on and telling others your story, and the way you experience others hearing it, actually shapes the story and the very neural correlates, or networks, it represents."[9] God, who is the ultimate Triune relational community, hardwired us to be relational beings in his own image.

People have a deep hunger for a more relational understanding of themselves and others. Recently I was invited to give a lecture at the University of San Francisco Law School. I was expecting ten to twelve attendees, half of them Christians. Instead, nearly fifty law students filled the room, mostly skeptics, all to hear a pastor speak on the wilderness temptations of Jesus.

I proceeded to explain that life is messy. I talked about how we're pulled in different directions by a cacophony of competing voices, all demanding allegiance to the same things that tempted Jesus: the desire to be special, successful, and secure. I talked about the relational significance of listening to the voice of God in those wilderness moments, of listening meditatively and contemplatively, as the Christian mystics have taught.

I even related this posture of living to some new research in interpersonal neuropsychology and to a psychological strategy called "mindfulness" — a way of being fully present to the moment and to the people you are with.[10]

As I spoke, I cast a vision for human relating that was rooted in our deeper identity as image-bearers created in and for love. I wondered aloud what the implications might be for lawyers, who are often viewed as relationally deceptive and morally bankrupt.

After the lecture a professor approached me, and I prepared

myself to be corrected by a lawyerly diatribe. Instead, he thanked me repeatedly, saying that law professors are now discovering the importance of healthy relating and mindful presence in a world primarily motivated by politicking and posturing. "It just works," he said. "People respond better." He appreciated the connections to historic Christian faith, adding that Christians often seem to be, in his words, the "least mindful" and "most judgmental" people. Then he invited me to speak at the law school again in the future.

I was stunned.

But perhaps I shouldn't have been. After all, the biblical narrative includes many insights about our relational core, our fundamental relational conflict, and its ultimate relational restoration. And if all truth is God's truth, who's to say that leaders, scientists, physicists, psychologists, and even law school professors can't discover that same truth? Today's best thinkers are rediscovering the fact that we are relational to our core — storied beings whose narratives are meant to reflect God's master narrative.

A Grand Story Rooted in Relationship

The story for Christians, of course, begins with God — a relational God called "Trinity," existing forever in self-giving love. "God is a sort of continuous and indivisible community," said Basil of Caesarea (330-379).[11] And human beings were created "very good," in the image of this Trinitarian, relational God (Gen. 1:27), made in and for relationship with God, one another, and the entire creation.

Loving interdependence. Endless giving and receiving. This is what was supposed to be.

As the Story goes, the original "very-goodness" of relational human beings took a tragic turn when God's human partners, the crown of creation, rebelled. They rejected the honest, loving relationships God intended them to have and turned toward deception, denial, betrayal, blame-shifting, alienation, and other negative behaviors. In Genesis 3 we encounter classic dysfunctional relational strategies that continue to plague humankind today.

Just as the "disease" is relational, so is the ultimate cure. God comes in the flesh in order to bridge the gap, recapture the heart of his wayward Bride, and pave the way to ultimate reconciliation. God did not send a memo, a textbook, or a doctrinal statement. He sent his own Son in self-giving, self-sacrificial love. He sent Jesus not just to redeem hearts but to restore relationships and rebuild trust.

It's no surprise, then, that psychologists and neurobiologists are uncovering the tragic Grand Story in the form of broken neural pathways and strained attachment relationships, or that physicists, law professors, and others are stumbling onto truth that reveals the "true story of the whole world"[12] embedded in creation's DNA.[13] It's an encouraging and exciting time. And there is a direct challenge in it to us.

It's time we start leading from a posture of relational health and integrity, the way God designed us to lead.

Leading as We Were Created to Lead

The Christian Story asserts that we were designed in and for healthy relationships, and that most of the difficulty and complexity in human life can be traced to a fundamental break in our relationships with God and each other. The term "original sin" names a mystery that no one can deny: the world is a broken place. When a child emerges from the safety of her mother's womb, she is immediately thrust into a world of chaos and conflict, and she cannot avoid the disappointments and difficulties of human life.

From the Christian perspective, what psychologists and therapists call "healthy relating" actually redirects us to the Creator's original design. While therapy and psychological insight may help, they cannot ultimately heal us. The problem lies at the core of our being, in that fundamental relational brokenness the Christian Story describes so poignantly. Only in rediscovering the original blessedness of healthy relationships between God, humans, and God's other marvelous creatures can we can find wholeness once more. Relearning the dynamics of healthy relating changes couples, groups, and even large organizations.[14]

So much of the Exodus story, in which God liberated his people after centuries of slavery in Egypt, deals with the need to rebuild relationships. God's actions and laws challenged every aspect of Israel's way of relating to him and to one another on their wilderness journey. Perhaps that journey lasted so long because the Israelites, like us, doggedly resisted the deep change that was necessary.

Just as the Israelites needed a key leader like Moses to help them understand God's intentions for their life together, so we need pastors and leaders to continue to play a key role in that understanding today. Interestingly, the Bible describes Moses as "more humble than anyone else on the face of the earth" (Num. 12:3). Leaders set the relational tone. Not only do we speak to God's original relational design in our leading and preaching, but we live it out over a cup of coffee or in a pastoral counseling session or in a performance review. If we somehow hide our own humanity behind the veneer of competence or power, we lose our ability to lead. When we fail to lead from a posture of humility, we replay the tragic betrayal told in the original creation story. We live from fear, self-protection, and control instead of integrity, transparency, and trust.

Dan Allender writes, "This is the strange paradox of leading: *to the degree you attempt to hide or dissemble your weaknesses, the more you will need to control those you lead, the more insecure you will become, and the more rigidity you will impose — prompting the ultimate departure of your best people.*"[15] It is, indeed, a paradox, as Allender says, because most of us have heard that we should lead by exerting authority, by "never letting them see us sweat." What we really need to do is to *be human,* while at the same time challenging others to become fully human themselves.

I once spoke with a board member of a nonprofit who related her growing conflict with the CEO, who was also chair of the board. She had been pressing for more honesty amid several near-scandalous personnel situations in the organization. So she boldly and honestly pointed to a lack of trust in the leadership. She did not do it angrily or accusingly, but in a humble tone that made it a "we" issue rather than a "you" issue.

The response from the corporate leader was to circle the wagons and fight. At the next board meeting, the CEO stood before the group and lectured on loyalty, insinuating that any pushback or critique meant disloyalty. He set new policies, essentially shutting down any opportunity for honest board involvement. His choice of policy over relationship, without any admission of weakness or poor judgment, only served to demoralize the board, prompting resignations from some and fearful loyalty from others.

When we as leaders create work environments or congregations where fear or anxiety reign, we may gain allegiance and loyalty, but it will be blind allegiance, anxious allegiance, and perhaps even abusive allegiance. And the tragedy, of course, is that we once again play out the twisted and misguided plotline that humanity has been playing out for millennia — a plotline rooted in self-protective fear and control rather than humility and trust.

Leadership Implications

When we fail to lead in a way that mirrors God's original design for relationships, our pathological patterns of fear, self-protection, and control can become systematized, even institutionalized. I sometimes consult for organizations embroiled in these unhealthy patterns, and I see four main ways in which twisted forms of leadership play out:

- **Motivational leadership.** Leaders motivate people to achieve goals, but when motivation becomes an artificial technique that seeks to elicit a certain response, it dehumanizes. Consider the pastor of a large church who believes that keeping people positive and upbeat will contribute to a growing, thriving congregation. He majors in Sunday pep-talks and treats staff meetings like cheerleading sessions. While the results might appear positive for a time, this style has the psychological effect of creating an atmosphere where "never is heard a discouraging word," and only success and positivity are welcome. A gap forms between leader and followers. That gap eventually erodes trust and, paradoxically, erodes motivation.

- **Mechanical leadership.** Mechanical leadership relies on techniques. Some leaders continually devour the latest books on leadership structures and systems. Instead of honestly admitting fearfulness or difficulty, these leaders often hide their relational anxiety behind effective systems. But systems and organizations, while important, do not effect deep change, and constant system change often creates anxiety among others, eventually eroding trust. While carefully thinking through good systems is important for any organization, we must always be mindful of our human tendency to hide behind techniques.

- **Manipulative leadership.** Manipulative leadership is social Darwinism, the survival of the fittest in a dog-eat-dog world. Manipulative leaders use Pavlovian incentives to boost performance, often at the expense of honest relating. I once counseled an exhausted associate pastor whose senior pastor measured success by baptisms and attendance numbers. The senior pastor used guilt very effectively to motivate his staff and congregation to "do more for God." He even offered year-end bonuses to staff members who secured the most baptisms! Essentially, he reduced the gospel to a product to be sold rather than a treasure to be shared. Manipulative leadership often settles for an "ends justifies the means" methodology.

- **Moralistic leadership.** Moralistic leadership uses perceived moral authority to intimidate and to engender conformity. A pastor once called me to challenge the way I was counseling a married couple in his congregation. After some spiritual pleasantries ("Hello, brother! I pray God is blessing you today"), he proceeded to recite a few carefully chosen Bible verses that were meant to dispute my approach. His purpose was not to discuss or consult, but to force change through moral superiority. Because moralists give the impression that they are never wrong, those under their leadership constantly question themselves.

Surrendering Our Need to Manage Life

Each of these styles is an attempt to manage the world using a strategy rooted in control rather than in the sometimes risky, vulnerable way of leading with humility and transparency. Eugene Peterson's paraphrase of Romans 9 portrays the risks of leading by control:

Instead of trusting God, *they* took over. They were absorbed in what they themselves were doing. They were so absorbed in their "God projects" that they didn't notice God right in front of them, like a huge rock in the middle of the road. And so they stumbled into him and went sprawling. *(The Message)*

All unhealthy and dysfunctional styles of leadership have one thing in common: they're based in anxiety and control. Ronald Richardson describes a healthier model when he discusses the emotional system of churches:

> Emotional systems are like delicately balanced mobiles. Any movement by any one part of the mobile, toward or away from the center of gravity, affects the balance of the whole mobile. This is most true of the parts closest to the top of the mobile (the leadership), and only somewhat less true of the parts closer to the bottom.
>
> The churches that function the best have leaders who experience less threat around the normal unbalancing that occurs (acute anxiety) and feel safer in the midst of the erratic movement of the mobile, while staying in touch with all parts of the mobile. The closer to the top of the mobile these calmer leaders are, the greater the calming effect they will have on the whole congregation. The more threatened and unsafe the leaders feel generally (chronic anxiety), the more the whole congregation can be disrupted.[16]

As we follow God's design and live into the relational vision that God hardwired into creation, we'll find that those moments of anxiety and fear will lift. Sure, we'll continue to struggle. But we'll struggle honestly and authentically, in community and in the presence of a God who invites us to risk living as mature adults and healthy human beings. And as we live into this vision, we may not only avoid burnout — we might just begin to experience the joy of leading difficult people like ourselves.

understanding our story

We would rather be ruined than changed,
We would rather die in our dread
Than climb the cross of the moment
And let our illusions die.

W. H. AUDEN

Despite everything you have achieved, life refuses to
grant you, and always will refuse to grant you, immunity
from its difficulties.

DAVID WHYTE

The Life-Light was the real thing:
Every person entering Life
he brings into Light.
He was in the world,
the world was there through him,
and yet the world didn't even notice.
He came to his own people,
but they didn't want him.
But whoever did want him,
who believed he was who he claimed

and would do what he said,
he made to be their true selves,
their child-of-God selves.

JOHN 1:9-12 (*THE MESSAGE*)

I N ONE WAY or another, we all mirror the ancient creation story. Our lives begin in a garden, but we soon find ourselves in a wilderness "east of Eden" (Gen. 3:24). From the comfort, safety, and security of our mother's womb, we emerge into a world where we cannot avoid failure, disappointment, and anxiety.

Country pastor and poet George Herbert wrote, "I cried when I was born and every day shows why."[1] To leave the idyllic paradise of the womb is, indeed, a jolt. Having watched my wife give birth to two little girls, I can tell you that our babies were not amused when they emerged into the cold air and bright lights! But almost immediately they discovered safety in their mother's arms.

At the moment of birth, the battle begins, and it's filled with tears and joy, fear and safety. As a parent, you try to do your best to mirror God's unconditional love. But the truth is, you'll fail.

I remember the first time that Emma, my sweet little first-born daughter, rolled off the ottoman I was changing her on when I reached for a diaper. I had determined to be an attentive father, always attuned to my children's needs. But, as a favorite poet of mine says, "Despite everything you have achieved, life refuses to grant you, and always will refuse to grant you, immunity from its difficulties."[2] Despite my achievements and determination, I've blown it time and again.

We cannot protect our children perfectly. Nor should we. Growth requires stumbling, falling, and getting up again. We learn by being told what not to do, but we also learn by making mistakes despite what we're told. This is true of both children and parents. We all fall, we all fail, and we all grow in the process. Richard Rohr writes, "The English mystic Julian of Norwich said, 'First the fall, and then the recovery from the fall, and both are the mercy of God.' It is in the falling down that we learn almost everything that matters spiritually."[3]

No child emerges from childhood unwounded. To be sure, there are the significant wounds of abuse, abandonment, and neglect. These are brutal for the human soul. However, even the best-raised children have to learn to cope. They, too, need to discover strategies for surviving life's curveballs.

In this chapter I offer a rather basic and straightforward paradigm for understanding people, one of the keys of which is to understand the early process of navigating life's twists and turns.

A Beautiful Complexity

Over the years, it has helped me immensely to learn that people are more beautifully complex than I had realized. In my simplistic theological framework earlier in life, I figured that people sin, that sin is bad, and that human repentance is the way out. But God has created us far more elaborately! Psychology reveals this in vivid color, but Scripture tells the story too.

When the psalmist said, "For you created my inmost being; you knit me together in my mother's womb" (Ps. 139:13), he was saying that our lives begin, like that ancient creation story, in a Garden — in perfect goodness. Theologians call it "original goodness," and it necessarily precedes "original sin." Without original goodness, we'd be missing that extraordinary key to human identity: the image of God. It's what constitutes us as relational and purposeful human beings. We're relational in that we mirror the Trinity, God-in-relationship. We were made male and female (Gen. 1:27), in and for community, to become lovers of God and neighbor.[4]

Being created in the image of God also conveys a sense of dignity in both our identity and our task. We are royal ambassadors of the King, called to announce and live out God's benevolent reign in the world.[5] That is good news. And that is more original than anything else about us.

The implications of this truth are huge for those of us who pastor or lead people. No matter how significant our struggle with another human being, we must never look at that person without remembering his or her original identity and purpose. Yes, this includes the most difficult people you lead:

- the woman who sits in the front row at your church taking notes, then sends a Monday-morning e-mail with all of her critiques;

- the whiny employee always looking for a raise or a compliment or another day off;

- the partner who betrayed you, leaving your business with half your clients and most of your investment.

God formed us in his image — a glorious thought! — but we all participate in the abandonment of that original identity. The biblical story of Adam, Eve, and the serpent is a familiar one, even if you've never read the biblical text. You know it because you've lived it. I've lived it. We've all heard the voice that says, "Surely you'd be more satisfied with [fill in the blank: knowledge, success, good looks, wealth] than with what God has given." We trade in our original design for a cheap imitation, though we don't always know it at the time.

Does that mean that your precious little child is a dirty rotten sinner, as some theologians might say? Certainly not. That would be another adventure in missing the point. As the venerable old Heidelberg Catechism puts it, "God created them [children] good and in his own image" (Q.& A. 6). But yes, every child is somehow caught up in the great mystery of the world's corruption: we are born into an unavoidably beautiful and broken world and become beautiful and broken ourselves. Adam and Eve's story becomes our story.[6] James Finley explains how this works:

> On the one hand there is the great truth that from the first moment of my existence the deepest dimension of my life is that I am made by God for union with himself. The deepest dimension of my identity as a human person is that I share in God's own life both now and in eternity in a relationship of untold intimacy. On the other hand, my own daily experience impresses upon me the painful truth that my heart has listened to the serpent instead of to God. There is something in me that puts on fig leaves of concealment, kills my brother, builds towers of confusion, and brings cosmic chaos upon the earth. There is something in me that loves darkness rather than light, that rejects God and thereby rejects my own deepest reality as a human person made in the image and likeness of God.[7]

This is our universal and personal story. But how does it all unfold?

From the very beginning, God "knits together" a child designed to ceaselessly receive and respond. Without her knowing it, a newborn's brain is wildly active, processing the complex world she's been welcomed into. But she doesn't realize that she's been born into a scary world, that she's inherited the best and the worst of Mom and Dad, that she's caught up in the beauty and the brokenness from the start. Mom and Dad do their very best, given the child's unique temperament, to provide love, safety, nurture, shelter, and sustenance. But they themselves are victims of the same brokenness.

These early interactions are, in fact, the most important interactions we'll ever have. It's hard to stake one's health and wholeness in life on a particular event or time period, but this is as close as we come to a make-or-break moment. Our first attachment to our primary caregivers sets the tone for the rest of our lives. Our early experiences, particularly traumatic experiences, create a lasting impact:

> A childhood replete with suffering lingers in the mind as bitter, encoded traces of pain. Even a tangential reminder of that suffering can spur the outbreak of unpleasant thoughts, feelings, anticipations. As if he had bumped a sleeping guard dog, the adult who was an abused child may feel the fearsome jaws of memory close after he glimpses a mere intimation of his former circumstances.[8]

Attachment theorists have taught us that as we grow, our style of relating emerges from these important early childhood relationships. They speak of children being either securely or insecurely attached, and we see it every day in our relationships with our family members, our employees, even our congregations.

An insecurely attached child learns to relate to the world in several ways. First, she may relate in an *anxious/ambivalent* way, finding it difficult to leave Mom's side, or get on the school bus, or do tasks on her own. At the same time, she isn't easily comforted when she's back in the presence of her parent. As an adult, she may be insecure in relationships, worrying if she's loved, and always fearful of loss. We all know people who are constantly looking for reassurance from us.

Second, she may relate in an *avoidant* way, showing little or no discrimination between a parent or a stranger. As an adult, she may show little capability for real connection or intimacy. Again, we all know people who go to their corners and don't make a lot of noise, but whose relational disconnection impacts the group.

Finally, she may relate in a *disorganized* way, showing a vacillating pattern of connection and withdrawal. Often, this style shows up as an overly parental or helpful posture she takes toward others as an adult, much to the neglect of her own emotional needs. We all know the helper who shows up to volunteer, who offers herself for every task, but who seems lonely and empty herself.

Most psychologists believe that securely attached individuals, by contrast, show a healthy ability to both connect to and be apart from Mom and Dad as a child. They are able to separate and become their own individual selves as they grow older. As adults, they are able to relate healthily, neither inordinately needing attention, reassurance, and approval, nor self-protectively avoiding relationships. Nurtured among secure individuals, these men and women can relate healthily, securely, and maturely.

I'm reminded of the importance of these insights every time I try to "fix" someone I'm attempting to help. I'm prone to offer some good advice, or maybe a behavioral strategy or two — not, in and of itself, a bad thing. But what we know now is that how we relate is much more complicated, that we're not dogs that can be quickly trained, but human beings shaped in the matrix of relationships. Curt Thompson describes this relational matrix by saying that "the way we attach shapes the neural networks that are the vehicles of the attachment process itself. Those neural networks then reinforce the same interpersonal dynamics, which leads us to attach to others in much the same way as we did to our parents."[9]

Knowing this relational complexity, wouldn't it make sense for us to practice a bit more curiosity when we deal with others? Instead of fixing the people we lead, wouldn't it make sense to take the time to get to know them?

Looking at Our Lives

Since the world is a relationally complex and maddening place, we all inevitably find both good and unproductive ways to navigate through it. And whether we're securely attached or not, we can't help but play the original game of Adam and Eve, hiding ourselves when difficult situations confront us.

I see it in both my daughters, who are eleven and twelve. I think they're fairly healthy, but they can play their mother and me like a fiddle sometimes, simply by putting on different personalities for different situations. They aren't trying to deceive us; they're just being human. My hope is that they'll always stay connected to a secure center, their core identity in God modeled imperfectly in our relationship with them. But I know they'll struggle. Middle school brings acne, peer pressure, and all sorts of drama. But with secure and stable core selves, strong relationships, and a lot of grace from God, they will, I hope, be just like many of us: holy messes, beautiful strugglers, both sinful and sanctified.

However, some people never develop that stable core in early life. A case in point is a former client of mine I'll call Madeline.

In her early years, Madeline seemed confident and smart. She related fairly well to her friends, usually helping the underdog, often assisting her teachers. Adults in her life praised her apparent maturity and helpfulness. But a closer look at her life tells a more important story.

In therapy she recognized that in her earliest relationships with her mom and dad, she was usually left on her own. Both parents worked, and though she was confident that they loved her, she also had to learn to fend for herself. At times she felt as if she were the one raising her three younger siblings. Her self-reliance was born out of the need to keep the house in order during the frequent absences of her parents.

Madeline came to me for therapy because she was unhappy in her marriage. Her husband would say to her, "You're always mothering me. What happened to the woman I met — the fun-loving, sensitive, doting girlfriend I remember?" But Madeline didn't seem to know the answer. All she knew was that she often felt angry, as if everything in her home, her work, and her family life was hers alone to do. Though she put on a smile at church and even volunteered for many different causes, she thought, *I've got to do this because no one else will.*

It didn't take long for me to assess what was really going on. Madeline had lost track of her own needs long ago. Her parents cared for her deeply, but didn't quite know how to express their love. She internalized a sense of responsibility for herself and took control of her world. She unknowingly crafted elaborate "fig leaves" in her early years.

She realized that "a part of me died back then, a part of me that was a young and innocent and needy little girl." She tried to have some fun in college, and experienced her best years dating her now-husband Jeff. But she quickly fell back into her default *disorganized* attachment style, stuffing her own needs deep down and living with an excessively responsible relationship to others. Today she lives an unhappy life, feeling overly invested in the decisions of her husband and kids, unable to separate her happiness from theirs, often managing only a low-level anger and depression.

Like many of us, Madeline had parents who weren't bad or abusive. She needn't live her life looking for someone to blame. But her journey into maturity will require her to look at her life, to open herself to the narrative that formed her and that guides her.

The Long, Invisible Bag We Drag behind Us

The great poet William Wordsworth once wrote,

Heaven lies about us in our infancy!
Shades of the prison-house begin to close
Upon the growing Boy.[10]

The poet and author Robert Bly tells the story of our lives with a compelling metaphor: a story of "the long, invisible bag we drag behind us."[11] My version goes like this. Sometime early in our childhood, we begin to realize that the world can be a difficult place. Mom says to us, "Ben, good boys don't get angry," or Dad says, "Elise, you can't leave the house with your hair like that. What will people think?" Or, in Madeline's case, our parents are too busy to say much to us at all. Mom and Dad aren't actively trying to hurt us, but as kids we're not privy to their larger perspective. So Ben puts his anger in an "invisible bag" where he stuffs all of his not-so-pleasant experiences — parts of himself he doesn't want the world to see. Perhaps Elise puts a bit of her free-spiritedness in the bag. And Madeline puts her young, innocent, fun-loving, and attention-starved self in the bag as she concentrates on keeping her parents and siblings happy.

Each story is different. We put in the bag what our families, our friends, and our culture deems unacceptable.

By high school, the invisible bag has grown quite a bit. The pressures of late elementary and middle school have caused these now-teenagers to stuff large parts of themselves away. They've developed a significant internal split. The so-called "bad" is tucked away, and the so-called "good" becomes the public persona. What their earliest caregivers approved of is valued, and what was not approved of is swept under the carpet. As psychologist and spiritual theologian David Benner says, "At some point in childhood we all make the powerful discovery that we can manipulate the truth about ourselves."[12] In a mysterious combination of conscious choosing and subconscious coping, we develop an acceptable persona, a false self that keeps our deeper, hidden self protected from the disapproval of others.

For most of us, even the most well-adjusted among us, by the time we find ourselves near midlife, our bag has become heavy. In our demanding world of relationships, jobs, spiritual expectations, and — well, the list goes exhaustingly on — we've learned to play the game. Different parts of us rise to the fore in different situations. We're often so unfamiliar with or ignorant of our true selves that we're out of touch with our deepest being.

Then perhaps we hear a hint of life-as-it's-meant-to-be in a sermon or a book, and our hearts stir. For a moment we're aware that life is larger, that our hearts run deeper. Even if it's just an echo from a distant and unfamiliar land, it's something. Frederick Buechner says it well:

> Life batters and shapes us in all sorts of ways before it's done, but those original selves which we were born with and which I believe we continue in some measure to be no matter what, are selves which still echo with the holiness of their origin. I believe that what Genesis suggests is that this original self, with the print of God's thumb still upon it, is the most essential part of who we are and is buried deep in all of us as a source of wisdom and strength and healing which we can draw upon or, with our terrible freedom, not draw upon as we choose.[13]

Midlife requires us to look inside the bag if we haven't yet. By then, life has become all too complicated. Age brings the reality of withering youth — wrinkles, aching muscles, decreasing resilience. Some who want to marry remain single, and some who are married would prefer the freedom of singleness. Debts grow. Children grow. And expectations only rise: "Save. Invest. Work hard. Get a raise. Lose weight. Fix your relationship." No wonder it's called midlife *crisis*.

For Madeline, the break came when she had her third child. Exhausted by the demands of her many volunteer activities and the rigors of being a mom, she lashed out at her husband and at life one day, exclaiming, "I quit!" Fortunately, Jeff was a fairly securely attached individual who saw her declaration as a step in the direction of freedom. He'd seen me for therapy himself, and was working hard on his own responses and reactivity in his marriage. So he responded well. He encouraged Madeline to go ahead and quit for a week or so. Then he encouraged her to see me for counseling.

At that point, Madeline had a choice to make. Either she could open the invisible bag and explore her forgotten self, or she could ignore the bag and continue to live out of a false self. In fact, we all have that choice. Opening the bag brings freedom and wholeness. We may discover that our burnout or depression or anxiety is due, in large part, to losing that forgotten true self. When the true self begins to emerge again, we begin to relate to God with an honesty that breaks down walls and allows resurrection life to surge within us. With King David we can declare, "Create in me a pure [undivided] heart, O God" (Ps. 51:10).

If we refuse to open the bag, whether out of fear or despair, we create more distance between us and God and between ourselves and others. We hear nothing but dissonance in our souls. Poet W. H. Auden ominously describes this fateful choice many of us make:

We would rather be ruined than changed,
We would rather die in our dread
Than climb the cross of the moment
And let our illusions die. [14]

This is the unexamined life. We roll the dice, hoping our relationships don't die and our careers don't self-combust.

Twentieth-century monk and prolific writer Thomas Merton said that every one of us is "shadowed by an illusory person: a false self." What is tragic is that this false and private self

> wants to exist outside the reach of God's will and God's love . . . and such a self cannot help but be an illusion. Thus I use up my life in the desire for pleasures and the thirst for experiences, for power, honor, knowledge, and love, to clothe this false self and construct its nothingness into something objectively real. But there is no substance under the things with which I am clothed. [15]

With a little courage, though, we can open the invisible bag. Perhaps we'll do it with a friend, a spouse, or a therapist, discovering inner resources we did not know we had, all originally bestowed in God's image in us. Perhaps our epiphany will come in Christian worship, in the liturgical rhythms of confession and communion, or through the better vision communicated in the Word, where we are reminded of our real identity and purpose.

The "long, invisible bag" is a metaphor that helps you and me recognize that we do have a story, a story written in the unique context of our families and communities, and yet a story that makes sense only in light of the Grand Story. To open the bag is not to engage in some empty, therapeutic technique for the sake of self-realization. No, we're invited to look at our lives in light of God's Story. We're invited to ask ourselves these questions:

- How do I hide?

- What is my unique set of fig leaves?

- What about my particular upbringing contributed to this one-of-a-kind set of fig leaves?

- Can I believe that God really wants to see and know me, all of me, even the darkest parts?

- What curiosity stirs with regard to others and how they hide?

- Am I prompted to greater compassion for others' stories?

God calls us, both individually and within our church communities, to this extraordinary work.

After they sinned, God greeted Adam and Eve in the Garden with the words "Where are you?" And the Spirit asks this same question of us, as well as the people we lead. Indeed, it takes a lifetime to answer. But God is committed to finding us, loving us, and restoring us for the sake of the beauty and blessing of his kingdom.

Part 2

LEADING AND LOVING DIFFICULT PEOPLE

personality disorders:
loving those who drive you crazy

The goal in handling dragons is not to destroy them, not
merely to disassociate, but to make them disciples. Even
when that seems an unlikely prospect.

MARSHALL SHELLEY

What I feared most of all was . . . the disaster of being
locked up in the dark of my own fear.

FREDERICK BUECHNER

Ministry kills us with regard to our ego needs, desire for
power and success, and the persistent wish to feel
competent and in control.

ANDREW PURVES

H AVING EXPLORED THE biblical story of the beauty and the
brokenness we inherit as human beings, we will now dig
deeper into one aspect of brokenness we often encounter in difficult
people: the messy realm of personality disorders. This is the term
that psychologists and psychiatrists use to describe certain clusters

of exceptionally severe relational patterns. The primary ones I see impacting leaders and pastors include the four listed below.

- Narcissistic Personality Disorder (NPD)

- Borderline Personality Disorder (BPD)

- Obsessive-Compulsive Personality Disorder (OCPD)

- Histrionic Personality Disorder (HPD)

Experts define a personality disorder as an "enduring pattern of inner experience and behavior that deviates markedly from the expectation of the individual's culture, is pervasive and inflexible, has an onset in adolescence or early adulthood, is stable over time, and leads to distress or impairment."[1] In theological terms, personality disorders reflect that long-term and chronic relational pattern Martin Luther describes as *homo incurvatus in se* — "people turned in on themselves."

People who are afflicted with personality disorders cannot relate as healthy image-bearers who give and receive love. Instead, they've developed twisted ways of getting what they need apart from God and through their own control. In the early church, theologians would talk of sin as disordered desire, emphasizing not so much the behavioral act of sin but the habitual patterns and passions which develop over time. We are talking about something very similar — patterns and habits which form over time, hijacking our deepest desire to love God and neighbor.

My first seminary counseling professor advised us that "people with personality disorders are what will drive many of you to leave ministry." Any pastor or other leader who has served for more than five years will tell you that people are the hardest thing about leadership, and that's especially true of people with personality disorders, such as

- the nagging parishioner who gives a lot but pesters you with daily e-mails asking for specific details about the organization's accounting. She is unable to see her own obsessiveness or to realize that her e-mails cause you anxiety and give you heartburn.

- the volunteer who spent years praising and supporting you, only to viciously turn on you, sending critical e-mails to everyone in the church.

- the music leader who seems to ooze drama and is a magnet for each and every crisis in your church.

- the power broker who intimidates you after you challenge him in a marital counseling session, demanding to see your notes from each session and threatening to get a lawyer to investigate you and the church.

- the leader who seemed so invested in and committed to your organization, only to be caught in sexual and financial infidelity, which rocks his family and explodes the trust and loyalty of the organization.

- the staff antagonist who seems to undermine your every decision, pairing off with others on your staff as she breeds mistrust and suspicion.

Whenever I describe these people in speaking engagements, I see pastors and leaders nodding with validation and seeming relief, recognizing that they aren't alone in their everyday struggles with broken men and women. I've seen leaders in tears sometimes, confessing to mood swings and anger, depression and sleeplessness, as they struggle to deal with disordered colleagues.

For years, experts believed that the prognosis for change among people who struggled with personality disorders was minimal, at best. Today a more integrated therapeutic approach brings new optimism.[2] Personality disorders will always require a significant amount of time for real change to occur. Unlike mood disorders such as depression or anxiety, personality disorders are deeply ingrained in one's character, often requiring therapy, prayer, spiritual discipline, and even medication. Yet in this chapter I hope to help by offering insights into how best to pastor, lead, and counsel people who suffer from personality disorders.

As Marshall Shelley wisely writes, as he reflects on the various "dragons" that pester pastors, "The goal in handling dragons is not to destroy them, not merely to disassociate, but to make them disciples. Even when that seems an unlikely prospect."[3] My reflections are merely introductory, but I hope they prompt you to greater hope, vision, wisdom, and compassion for people whom Jesus would welcome, love, and perhaps even call disciples.

My approach has sometimes been criticized by people within the church who feel I diminish the role of sin, as well as by those within the world of psychology who feel I emphasize sin and responsibility too much. My hope is that this approach will help us recognize that we're all a lot more complicated than we think, that we can be both victims and perpetrators, and that God's love is big enough both to heal our hurts and to forgive our sins. If we cannot have a vision for the most broken people among us, perhaps our cynical hearts are also in need of some healing.

The Narcissist

A narcissist (the word is derived from the Greek ναρκη ["numb"])
is one who has been robbed of a God-given desire to live for and
love others; instead, he is turned inward and enamored by his own
image. A narcissist, in other words, is a self-worshipper, numb to
his or her deepest (created) desire to love and be loved by God.[4]

He may be the image-driven salesman or the arrogant entrepre-
neur, the success-addicted pastor or the self-interested politician,
the PTA president or the Internet blogger. Narcissism comes in
many forms. He's generally self-assured and certain, polished and
professional. She's often bold and brazen, showy and strong. In
fact, my first hint that I'm in the presence of a narcissist is what I
might feel — sometimes envy, sometimes insecurity, at other times
a surge of power and dominance. Narcissists are experts at keeping
others feeling inadequate.

I remember the client I once saw while working at a seminary.
He parked his car, quite intentionally, in the President's parking spot
when it was open. He walked into the main doors with a confident
stride, shirt unbuttoned, gold chain and chest hair exposed, simply
ignoring those who greeted him. He called me "Doctor," paid in
cash only, and didn't want a receipt, because a paper trail might
be discovered, alerting others to the fact that he was in therapy.
However, while he complained of the many others in his life who
failed to live up to his standards (including me, I'm quite sure), he
could never really see beyond his tragically self-assured ego to the
vulnerable person inside.

As I pointed out in Part 1, so much of who we are emerges from
the way we adapt, self-protect, and cope with our early childhood
environments. This is particularly important to remember as we
explore the narcissist. Psychologist James Masterson theorizes that
"the narcissist's personality is based on a defensive false self that he

must keep inflated, like a balloon, in order not to feel the underlying rage and depression associated with an inadequate, fragmented sense of self."[5] The narcissist is never wrong — unless, of course, his acknowledgment of wrongdoing is a well-calculated way of manipulating a situation. Honestly acknowledging sin or failure would so fracture his ego that his life, as he knows it, could not continue.

The narcissistic personality is often seen in power brokers, whether in the church, politics, the media, or other prominent public arenas. When such a person takes a spectacular fall, we inevitably ask questions. How could it be that a presidential candidate like John Edwards might have an affair, and perhaps even misuse campaign funds, while his wife is suffering and dying? How could it be that a seemingly impregnable radio personality like Rush Limbaugh could be addicted to painkillers? The most powerful among us are often the most susceptible.

I see a combination of misguided power and low empathy in almost every narcissist I work with. Narcissistic men and women often feign empathy, appearing to be supportive of others, but ultimately acting only for their own good. They enter a room noticing the most powerful person in the room, only seeing him or her as a competitor who must be defeated. The narcissist in an organization or a church is often an influential person who plays the game of relationships well, appearing charming and interested. He approaches you at a meeting or church group and asks questions about you. But soon the gravitational force pulls towards him. He monopolizes time, appearing sincere at first but becoming increasingly self-serving as time goes on. She's optimistic, unless relating to people who she knows well (her husband, or an employee, or a child). In these cases, she can become condescending. In your group, he is interested and engaged until the tide turns in a direction he disagrees with; then he displays an anger that takes you by surprise.

In their ministry or leadership position, you find their personality compelling, until you experience their wrath. In friendships, they boast of their accomplishments, but rarely show interest in your life or struggles. They are disconnected from their own pain, insecurity, and fear. And ultimately, this is what narcissism reveals. While manifesting power, superiority, cynicism about failure, and a need to control, deep down narcissists cannot fail — in their work, relationships, or friendships. Underneath their powerful and impressive exteriors lies a deep insecurity. Of course, narcissists are completely unaware of this inner battle, and we can only pray they realize it in time.

Perhaps this description makes you feel somewhat hopeless. Can narcissists be helped? Can they change? Having worked with narcissists for sixteen years as a primary specialization in my counseling practice, I find that, unfortunately, some will never give up power for the sake of a vulnerable relationship where real honesty and humility can exist. Yet, I've also grown more hopeful over the years as I see the redemptive power of love bring substantial healing among those I've worked with.

First, those who struggle with a narcissistic personality can heal only *in community.* The wife who seeks to change an emotionally abusive and narcissistic husband on her own fights a losing battle. Because narcissists are so concerned about their image and their position in a community (or even within their extended family), pressure from that community can motivate them to change. That said, someone struggling with diagnosable narcissistic personality disorder will also require therapy.[6]

The church, as a loving but firm redemptive community, can also be a significant healing agent. Its worship, and especially the communion table, can be a place of welcome and healing for the narcissist who is able to see himself as a member of the community of people who are both broken and loved. Confession can be a weekly invitation to humility. Christians living as a cruciform community, shaped by Christ's life and death, challenge the arrogant pride of the narcissist (1 Cor. 1:18-31). For, in many respects, the narcissistic personality is antithetical to a cruciform Christian life.

Second, I've found that strongly confronting a narcissist, while sometimes necessary (particularly in cases where family members have been hurt or abused), is almost always counter-productive. The narcissist's false self is powerful precisely because he has experienced the negative powerlessness tightly contained in that invisible bag he drags behind him. Confrontation, though sometimes necessary, often leads only to defensiveness. The person considering confrontation needs to count the potential cost.

I find that a better approach entails sharing what I see and feel with the narcissist, modeling vulnerability. I see this as a kind of back-door appoach, a way of getting around the defensive ego to the vulnerable heart beneath. I once said to a particular client, "I find myself wanting to admire you, but I feel disconnected from you. I feel like you've set us up to be competitive, but I don't want to be. To be honest, I just want you to find one safe place where you don't have to be 'on.' Maybe we can have that." I've found often that men and women who struggle in these ways secretly long to shed the narcissistic posture for a taste of authentic connection. They have stories, like you and me. Many have been hurt in their early years, and have coped by becoming tough, powerful, and crafty. But I've found that the toughest customers are just too insecure and afraid to risk connection.

Reflecting honestly on his own life, pastor and author Frederick Buechner once wrote, "What I feared most of all was . . . the disaster of being locked up in the dark of my own fear."[7] It's helpful to know that wise souls like Buechner struggle too. We may give the appearance of strength and invincibility, but we all wear elaborate, self-protective masks. That's why we can all find hope and healing in a Savior who became weak so that we might find our strength and dignity in him.

Third, it is important to determine if a narcissist is able or willing to see the impact she has on others, even if only in part. I've found that even a small degree of self-awareness can go a long way, opening the doors for some deeper work in therapy, and some level of repentance. It is important to recognize the narcissist's "damage zone," as I call it, and call her to take responsibility for it. If the narcissist is a leader in a corporate setting, her collateral damage may lead to her termination. In the church, dealing with the narcissist is a bit more difficult. Pastors must have the courage to step into the mess, facing the damage a narcissist has done to his family, to the congregation, to the leadership, and to the church's reputation. I always find it easier to deal with a narcissist who has few connections to others and has caused little damage rather than one enmeshed within a community traumatized by him. Pastors have to weigh protecting the community and pursuing the perpetrator. This is one of the things that make pastoring so difficult.

Without some self-awareness and repentance on the narcissist's part, tough love will likely need to be applied. Having been involved in many sad cases of church discipline, I've often seen the necessity for a strong communal response to a particularly stubborn narcissist.[8] But for those who show even a small degree of self-awareness, a softer and more compassionate approach often works best.

Narcissists have the ability to sabotage your group, your church, or your organization. The question is, Will you avoid or ignore them, or will you step into the situation, giving them an opportunity to see their sin and own it, not through a power struggle but through a loving relationship? Although most narcissists will resist, I've also seen many who have not only recognized their own inner turmoil and its destructive effects, but have turned into extraordinary and humble people. Recall that narcissists' lack of empathy and penchant for power hide a very deep insecurity underneath. The invisible bag they drag behind them burdens their life. Recognize that very few people have had the courage or taken the time to be curious, to ask about their story or come close to them. And remember that, when a narcissist owns the burden of his load and its destructive consequences to others, repents, and begins to change, a new and humbled self emerges that has the capacity for genuine love and service.

God is in the business of redemption and restoration. When we relate to the narcissist in loving honesty, we join in God's redemptive work.

The Borderline

When the movie *Mommie Dearest* first appeared in theaters in 1981, many found their eyes opened to a psychological phenomenon once reserved for academic psychology. The movie portrayed the actress Joan Crawford, a wonderfully talented but psychologically complex mother, whose confusing inner life brought trauma to her son and daughter. The confusing "push-pull" dynamic came to life on the big screen. Many related to the brilliant portrayal of this disturbed mother who, on the one hand, showed lavish love to her children, and on the other, emotionally and physically abused them.

Certainly, any parent can relate to the alternate love and anger they feel toward their children, but the emotional swings of a borderline personality are far more drastic and intense. The DSM-IV, a psychologist's manual for understanding mental disorders, notes that "BPD is manifested by a pervasive pattern of instability of interpersonal relationships, self-image, and affects, and marked impulsivity beginning by early adulthood and present in a variety of contexts."[9]

It goes on to note that borderline behavior might be marked by a variety of things — frantic efforts to avoid abandonment, a pattern of unstable and intense interpersonal relationships, unstable self-image, impulsivity (e.g., spending sprees, casual sexual encounters, substance abuse, reckless driving, binge eating), recurrent suicidality, reactivity, chronic feelings of emptiness, inappropriate and intense, and perhaps even stress-related paranoia.

Because of the difficulty of working with this personality, I've heard some excellent clinicians over the years say, "I'll see almost anyone for therapy, but I refuse to see borderlines." The reason is that working with this personality can be exhausting. Boundaries can quickly become muddled. The drama can become intense.

A clearly diagnosable borderline will spend many years in therapy, with only incremental progress in most situations. And while medication can help some symptoms, the underlying psychic fracture only heals with time, and in a committed, safe relationship. Borderlines often show symptoms of self-destructive behavior — suicide attempts, cutting, binging and purging — all as ways of both hurting a part of them they hate, and gaining acceptance and reassurance among those who they imagine can rescue them. Thus, the borderlines' tragic stories require great patience, wisdom, prayerfulness, and compassion from us, even when they exhaust us.

Most pastors and leaders I know have grueling stories to tell about interactions with borderline personalities, though many lacked an understanding of what they were dealing with. One young pastor told me of a woman who came to his church filled with passion and energy. Divorced, she wanted to start a ministry for others like her. She filled the pastor's inbox with e-mails and voice-mails. To pacify her, he blessed her effort, allowing her to start a group. But when she gave him receipts for the group's activities after six months, he politely told her that the church hadn't agreed to financially support the group. She exploded in rage. Her e-mail to him was copied to the entire group, and many others in the church: "I came to you in a difficult time and self-sacrificially committed to helping others, but this is how you treat me?" Many in the congregation sided with her — some out of fear, others sucked into her passive-aggressive vortex. The woman would not relent, bringing up a host of other issues, and eventually prompting the young, inexperienced pastor to resign his pastorate.

And then there was a colleague and fellow professor who told me about a difficult student. The student was diligent and dutiful, sitting in the front row and offering to get coffee or snacks for the professor at breaks. That is, until the professor gave him a B on a mid-term exam. For the remainder of the semester, the student sat in the back, often distracted and distracting. On the final evaluation, the student wrote negative comments that questioned the competence and integrity of the professor.

If you lead an organization, a borderline personality can be your greatest source of confusion. You second-guess your responses. You hyper-evaluate your conversations. *Maybe I did do something wrong,* you think. But you haven't. In fact, you've given more than you should have to this person.

You know you're dealing with a borderline when you begin expending more time and emotional energy than you should on one person. You become caught up in e-mail exchanges that seem to have no end. You get roped into meetings that produce little resolution. And you feel like *you* are always the problem. This occurs because borderlines have experienced extraordinary pain and rejection at the hands of others, but they project that on to you. You begin as their savior, but quickly become another abuser. You become the father who rejected them. You become the mother who wouldn't listen. And, if you're not aware of this psychological interplay, you're quickly sucked into a vortex of frustration and futility.

As difficult as it is, there are ways to help borderline personalities, or at least to prevent ourselves from being swept into their twisted world.

First, most people react to a borderline personality through a fight-or-flight pattern. Some of us want to fight the borderline, hoping to match his or her aggressive behavior with our own; others run away. These are natural reactions. However, they only further convince the borderline personality that he or she is a "reject." Resist fight-or-flight, choosing instead a *compassionate* but *firm* relational engagement. This leads to the next insight.

Second, loving a borderline personality requires a certain emotional tenacity and even cunning. When I interact with a borderline, I imagine myself interacting with two people. One part of her requires compassion. It is that rejected and vulnerable part of the borderline who, like a little child, lives life fearfully and self-protectively. I can care for a borderline knowing she is fragile and requires compassion and love. However, there is the other part, the pathologic false self, which is trying to survive in the battlefield of life, grabbing love where she can get it and fighting away perceived rejection when she faces it. It is this confusing, passive-aggressive part of her that you need to confront empathetically, with the hope that she will begin to recognize her unhealthy and destructive ways of relating, and enter into a safe relationship where healing can occur.

Third, working with a borderline personality takes patience and wisdom. The leader will need not only to care for this person, but also *to protect others* from her. Helping the borderline calls for a kind of holy patience that requires prayer. Because such a person can wreak havoc on your church or organization, you may need to make hard choices. At times, wisdom dictates that you protect the other sheep from the predator. But the messy business of leading an organization or church requires you to resist your own desire to fight or flee, instead stepping into the situation both compassionately and carefully.

Finally, dealing with a borderline personality requires creating strong boundaries. Because he or she will demand a leader's time and energy like no other, you will need to set clear guidelines and stick to them. In a church or organization, you will likely need to limit the borderline's responsibilities, including his/her oversight of others, as well as limit the time he/she often demands. Remember that the borderline personality is hardly capable of healthy relationship, so a highly relational role will likely be destructive. It's wise to keep the boundary of your role foremost in the relationship, being fair but firm in parceling out your time. It is always fine to say, "I can't speak with you now, but I have fifteen minutes to talk later today. When can I call you?"

True borderline personalities may be the most exhausting people in your organization or church. At times you will find yourself filled with animosity toward them. But they are broken and hurting people, desperately in need of love and healing, a difficult task that will also cause you to grow and mature very quickly as a leader. They will teach you the importance of your boundaries as they stretch your patience and love.

The Obsessive-Compulsive

"Be perfect as God is perfect." This is the motto of the obsessive-compulsive.[10] With a penchant for criticizing and a gift for seeing things everyone else misses, the obsessive-compulsive is the ultimate Monday-morning critic.

You might receive an e-mail with a litany of concerns. On and on the e-mail goes, noting your failures, highlighting missed opportunities, asserting a message with a one-two punch of moralism and certainty that can be a knockout to a young pastor or leader.

I once chaired a denominational committee responsible for preparing potential candidates for pastoral ministry. During one meeting, I introduced a young candidate, saying, "I'd like you to meet John. I've known him for some time. He's a really good guy."

A member of our local presbytery stood and raised his hand, saying, "Point of personal privilege!" I was startled, but he continued, saying to me, "Brother, can we say that anyone is good?" I was speechless. He wasn't merely attempting to correct my theology, to make sure that I knew that people were *totally depraved,* as the Calvinist doctrine goes. He was projecting his own demanding sort of perfectionism on the young candidate. Part of me wanted to respond sarcastically, even angrily. Yet another part felt great sadness for this man, who obviously lives in a perfectly ordered internal world where these corrections *feel* necessary, and where his theology is more developed than his relational maturity.

Obsessive-Compulsive Personality Disorder (OCPD) manifests in the person who has constructed his world around order and control. He refuses to open that long, heavy, invisible bag of his own struggles, which is likely filled with chaotic emotions and deep doubts about his own perfection. This makes it especially difficult to provide honest and critical feedback, because he sees criticism as an indictment of sorts — a sign of weakness, failure, or imperfection — something that his psyche vigorously defends against. Indeed, this person can put up an impressive defense — lawyerly, tightly argued, airtight. The defenses which protect the vulnerable soul's interior are powerful.

If you are a leader, an obsessive-compulsive person will work hard, but that productivity will come with a cost. I was talking to a CEO recently who remarked that a particular employee was both brilliant and brutal. He loved his employee's tenacity, but loathed his constant barrage of criticism. Eventually, he sacrificed the man's contribution to the company for his own sanity. Another leader recently fired a very competent lawyer because he was simply tired of the man's constant compulsive criticism.

The obsessive-compulsive personality can manifest itself in a kind of moralism that sees the faults in everyone else. It can also manifest itself in a penchant for certainty that refuses to acknowledge life's gray areas. Or it displays a perfectionism which makes everyone else around feel uneasy and inadequate. Leaders with this disorder tend to be performance-driven and tyrannical. Among Christians and in the church, this personality displays a theological arrogance which demonizes all who don't "get it" (a posture seen among both liberals and fundamentalists). Some obsessive-compulsives resort to organizational filibustering in an attempt to stall processes and prevent change they see as wrong.

So, how do we deal with the obsessive-compulsive in a way that is both compassionate and helpful?

Once again, it's best not to engage in hard-hitting confrontation, which will only incite the person's defenses. Remember that beneath the controlled exterior is a fearful little child, rigidly managing life to protect himself from weakness, pain, and chaos.

Next, recognize that the obsessive-compulsive's worldview is so geared to control, emotional regulation, and stability that you'll need to tread slowly and patiently into his inner world, gaining trust along the way. You do not gain trust by the use of techniques, but in and through relationship. I find that a person will relinquish control only when he or she feels safe.

While I make it a priority to develop a relationship in which the obsessive-compulsive can trust me and thus surrender his or her control in my presence, I may also employ tools which encourage the process. One way that I have tried to do this is by inviting people to watch movies, movies which I hope will get beneath the surface and help them to see their disordered and impossible demands on themselves and others.[11] (For obsessive-compulsives, just allowing themselves the freedom to watch movies is in itself an act of repentance, a choice to relax rather than to churn and obsess.) At some point after that, I will then seek to engage them in a discussion to see if anything connected with them personally.

I have also suggested a reading or two on the latest brain research, highlighted in Chapter 1, or on emotional intelligence, which conveys in a logical way how important it is to engage relationally, empathetically, and emotionally with others. An obsessive-compulsive tends to respond more to clear, logical analysis than feeling-oriented discussion. I remember a particular client who was grateful to know that the best research-based insights suggest that human flourishing is much larger than intellectual assent or ethical living, but intersects with one's emotions, story, and even with one's shame. With a wry smile, he said, "Chuck, this makes me quite uncomfortable to acknowledge, but the research suggests that I need to grow up!" We both laughed, and new hope was born out of this experience.

Another way I go about encouraging the inner growth of someone who is obsessive-compulsive is by sharing my own story. In particular, I'll often offer the story of how I worked tirelessly to gain acceptance to Oxford University, only to recognize in the end that my "acceptance" did nothing to curb the deep inadequacy I felt. Each of us has a story of striving to succeed, only to see the impossibility of achieving deep satisfaction. Each of us has a self-righteous side, pining for approval like the elder brother in the Parable of the Prodigal Son (Luke 15). It's always important to recognize the great fear an obsessive-compulsive lives with every day. Though he appears strong and impenetrable, a very scared, out-of-control child hides inside, desperately needing to know that the world is safe, that he is acceptable, and that it will be OK. Sharing one's own personal stories can be a powerful way to connect with these fears, insecurities, and failed strivings.

Finally, it's the message of grace that will penetrate the armor of the obsessive personality. The central message that God accepts in Christ by grace alone is what this person longs to hear, but finds so difficult to believe. Most obsessive men and women live in their heads, where the Gospel is a believed truth but not an experienced reality. I've often found myself recommending the works of writers like Henri Nouwen, Brennan Manning, Jean Vanier, and others who've taught me about a lived grace. And I've often recommended disciplines of silence and solitude, contemplative prayer and lectio readings of Scripture, the Ignatian Examen, and other forms of intentionally restful presence with God.

Perhaps it takes a lifetime to believe the remarkably rest-inviting words of Jesus: "My yoke is easy, and my burden is light" (Matt. 11:30).

The Histrionic

The word "histrionic" comes from the Latin word that means "actor." It is not strange, then, that a histrionic lives her life onstage. For the person with Histrionic Personality Disorder (HPD), life is a drama, and the pervasive pattern of the histrionic personality is an emotional roller-coaster lurching between comedy and tragedy, lived out before your very eyes. With a major need for approval, a histrionic can be overly enthusiastic and even flirtatious, an alluring combination which the leader ought to be very mindful of.[12]

I recall one young woman who begged me to allow her to be on the worship team at the church. Sometimes she approached me in tears; at other times, she attempted a more subtle and seductive demeanor. Truth be told, she had no musical talent. She merely loved the stage. But, of course, she disagreed, and felt deeply hurt by my refusal to allow her to join the team. But, alas, she would find her way to the second or third row on Sundays, not far from me, so that I could hear her loud but pitchless voice, yet again trying to convince me of her talent.

What I often tell my counseling students is that you've broken through the dramatic false self of the histrionic when you see her "backstage" self, without the makeup, the antics, the false tears or false laughter. This is a sacred privilege if you've experienced it, as it is very rare with someone who is diagnosably histrionic. I remember sitting up in my chair, leaning in, and peering intently into the eyes of one woman I had seen for several years in counseling, saying, "Is that really you?" She had left the stage, and I saw her, perhaps for the first time, without her mask.

An individual develops a histrionic personality as a way of compensating within his or her childhood environment. It might manifest in an only child who is constantly the center of attention or is expected to behave like a "little man" or a "big girl." Or a histrionic is the child of addicts, in the middle of daily soap operas between fighting parents. Sometimes a histrionic is a child of highly successful parents, always on display to his parents' friends. At other times the histrionic personality develops in a child who desperately wants attention from passive, neglectful parents. Or it may develop in a child who feels she needs to compete for attention within a large family with many siblings. The child develops this personality in an attempt to navigate his or her early world. He or she develops a false self early on, stuffing into the invisible bag anything that he or she considers boring, mundane, or ordinary, and presenting only the public self, masked for display.

Working with and helping a histrionic personality requires a leader to be able to see both the stage self and the backstage self. While the stage self may dazzle you, or annoy and frustrate you, the backstage self is needy, hurting, and clearly desperate for attention. When I see a histrionic personality for therapy, it soon becomes clear that she wants to be my most special and important client. She works hard to make herself memorable. This is tragic and heartbreaking, for beneath this posturing lies the deeper story of sadness and loss.

A good friend, mentor, or leader is one who seeks to help the histrionic personality know and own her whole self. While you recognize some of the gifts of the masked stage actor, you do not seek to use or exploit these gifts. In other words, while it may be compelling to give this person a role on the worship team or with the prayer ministry or on the marketing team, you recognize that this might be ultimately destructive. With vision and with wisdom, you pave a new and different way, which invites the histrionic to live more wholly — perhaps in a less public role, one where she can serve others humbly, quietly, and self-sacrificially.

Like dealing with others with personality disorders, dealing with the histrionic may mean setting appropriate boundaries for her, since her seductive, invasive, or reassurance-demanding nature can quickly put us in an awkward, if not unethical, situation. With histrionic women, it's important to recognize that their often seductive behavior comes from being overly sexualized since their youth. And if you are a man working with a woman, you will want to make sure she feels cared for in a situation that provides safety and dignity. The last thing she needs is either to feel dangerous, often prompted by our fear and guilt, or to feel sexually or emotionally needed, often prompted by our own emotional immaturity. Without these clear boundaries, developing a close, helping relationship with a histrionic personality across sexual lines can lead to tragedy.

Finally, providing a safe place for the backstage personality to emerge is crucial in helping the histrionic personality. Do not give up on her, on the one hand, or *use* her stage talents on the other. See her through the eyes of Jesus, who seemed to cut through the masks and recognize the heart, often asking, "What do you really want?" (Mark 10:51). The histrionic wants to be known and loved for who she really is, not the stage self she presents.

A Challenge for Us

As we've examined each personality disorder in this chapter, we've seen that what we often simply call "sin" has its source in a lifelong, complex relational pattern. Learning to love people with these disorders takes a long time, as we find that we tend to give up, become cynical, or turn inward ourselves. The greatest and wisest leaders will lovingly and carefully engage with these broken colleagues, friends, and congregants, facing their fears, enduring the difficulties, and learning about themselves in the process. Wise leaders and pastors are forged in the crucible of these most difficult relationships. Andrew Purves could just as well be talking about leadership in general when he writes in his wonderful work *The Crucifixion of Ministry,* "Ministry kills us with regard to our ego needs, desire for power and success, and the persistent wish to feel competent and in control."[13]

Throughout this chapter I have described people in terms of the labels placed on them by professionals over the years. It's crucial to remember that no one can be reduced to a label, although labels often help us to understand and aid others. As a colleague reminded me, "Labels are helpful when they broaden our ability to understand and empathize with a person. They are destructive when they confine us and cause us to see the person more narrowly."[14] Each person is an image-bearer of God, created in and for a relationship with God and others, and a purpose in God's kingdom. To the extent that we maintain this vision, not only will we love the "least of these," but we will be given the energy and wisdom necessary to walk through the relational wilderness with others, even when they bring us to the edge of our resources. It's precisely there that we will discover that we're broken too, loved and pursued despite our best attempts at sabotage, by a God who dares to keep moving toward us, and propelling us out toward others.

addictions: loving in the dark

Addiction goes deeper than obsession and compulsion. It
is worship. It is giving my heart and soul over to something that I believe will ease my pain and provide an
outlet for my fury at being out of control in a world that
hurts me, scares me, or leaves me alone.

SHARON HERSH

To be alive is to be addicted, and to be alive and addicted
is to stand in need of grace.

GERALD MAY

Ruin has caused me to ruminate.

SHAKESPEARE

O F ALL THE DIFFICULT TYPES of people we deal with in our
organizations or churches, we are certain to encounter the
addict. And to begin understand the addict, its necessary to begin
with ourselves. As the late psychiatrist and spiritual director Gerald
May once said, "To be alive is to be addicted, and to be alive and
addicted is to stand in need of grace."[1]

Once, when I was quoting this assertion at a men's retreat, one attendee yelled out, "Sounds like the psychiatrist himself was a quack!" May's words are jolting. As we look at the substance abuser who has snorted away his life, we may feel contempt or pity, but not self-discovery.

We may not be addicts — we may be worse. In the upside-down economy of Jesus, those closest to the bottom are nearest to grace. Polished and put together, many of us live our lives without a real, palpable need for God. We preach grace. But we're working really, really hard to avoid hitting bottom ourselves.

Desperately trying to make our way in an often chaotic world, we clench our hands around anything and everything that provides some semblance of security. We hold tightly to our wallets and our reputations. We measure our status by Twitter followers and job titles. No, we're not high as a kite, but we're no better off.[2] In fact, if you take the words of Jesus seriously, the religiously put-together, the rich, and the secure are far less apt to beg for grace. And readers — that's most of us.

Bill Plotkin says it well in his provocative book *Soulcraft*: "The Western worldview says, in essence, that technological progress is the highest value and that we were born to consume, to endlessly use and discard natural resources, other species, technological gadgets, toys, and, often, other people."[3] If Plotkin is right, we're not simply making an idol here or there, whether it be an idol of success or an idol of beauty. Rather, addiction is happening at the level of our society, impacting our very identities. As the authors of *Hope in Troubled Times* write,

> People elevate something they themselves have fashioned to an exalted position in society (representation). Next, people make sacrifices on this idol's behalf, as if it possesses its own life and power (veneration). Finally, decision-makers and citizens follow it wherever it leads (transformation),

even if over the course of time the original end fades or seems no longer achievable.[4]

If these authors are right, what we fashion into an idol has the power to eventually hold us in its thrall, at a societal level and at a personal level. We're all far more addicted than we know, and far more in need of grace than we think.

The Powerlessness in Helping

That's an important starting point. And I think it's a necessary one if you're going to help an addict. It is important to know your own deep need for God in order to meet an addict honestly and compassionately. But, even still, working with an addict is never, ever easy.

In sixteen years of counseling and pastoral ministry, I have counseled alcoholics and sex addicts, self-mutilators and bulimics, trichotillomaniacs and potheads. I've done clinical counseling, but as a pastor I've also had to do funerals. I remember sitting with the mother of a 21-year-old drug addict who had overdosed; she cried in my arms, repeating, "Why? Why? Why?"

In my second year of ministry, a leader in our church and in business set up an appointment with me. He was a man I respected — intelligent, wise, self-sacrificial. I remember that day, because the tears flowed as he shared decades of failed attempts to get his beloved sister help for her out-of-control addictive lifestyle. She was living under a bridge downtown, and he wondered if he should once again "rescue" her. He felt powerless, unable to make this critical decision himself. Should he rescue her again, or let her go? We all stand in need of grace as we care for the addict, as we're brought to our knees time and again.

What does a pastor or therapist do in situation like this one? Who feels wise enough or prepared enough to make these life-or-death decisions? Even with a counseling degree, I certainly didn't. This man's sister had been through years of rehab. She'd stay sober for a while but then relapse, over and over again, dashing her family's hope for any sort of stability. But now her brother was asking me to make the decision for him. How do we advise people in these situations?

A related question is this: How do leaders navigate the messy terrain of managing someone who struggles with addiction? How does a CEO deal with his gifted VP's pornography addiction, an addiction that sucks up time and energy, and violates company policy?

I don't know about you, but with years of training and experience, I still experience some level of powerlessness in these moments. I admit that, hoping you'll allow yourself the freedom to *not* have all the answers, though I hope to give you some direction. One thing is inevitable — you'll make mistakes along the way. You'll be too compassionate at certain times, and too hard at others. You'll react too quickly at one moment, and avoid and even enable at another. Indeed, you'll need care and counsel for yourself along the way, particularly in very messy cases. But I pray you'll feel the grace to love imperfectly, and find the courage to keep trying.

Addiction as an Identity Problem

The fundamental reality I begin with when caring for or counseling anyone, including the addict, is that she was created in and for deep and lasting union with God. In Chapter 2, I described this reality as the "image of God," God's originally good imprint on our lives that gives us our identity and our mission in the world. But let's take it a step further.

This image represents God's original union with us. We were made in and for relationship, for union and communion with God, one another, and God's blessed creation. This is the "you" that each of us has. It is the you that God knit together, the you known personally and intimately by God, your true self.

But, as we've said, we're thrust into a world where our deepest craving for union is subverted in a thousand ways. While God is our most deep and original Desire, our hearts long for connection, security, and control. Left to navigate our messy worlds, we search for something — anything — which will soothe the ache. We seek what theologians call "attachment," something or someone to place our identity in, to help us feel secure, to give us some measure of control. Attachment is the breeding ground of addiction.

Addiction is an attempt to master reality on our own terms, a refusal to live in the world God has made. And our desire for control is at the heart of it. Our restless hearts demand satisfaction — *now*. We refuse to wait. We refuse to hunger. We refuse to thirst. Created with a relentless desire for God, we attach that desire to something else, something more manageable, more controllable. Gerald May writes,

> Addiction exists wherever persons are internally compelled to give energy to things that are not their true desires. To define it directly, addiction is a state of compulsion, obsession, or preoccupation that enslaves a person's will and desire. Addiction sidetracks and eclipses the energy of our deepest, truest desire for love and goodness. We succumb because the energy of our desire becomes attached, nailed, to specific behaviors, objects, or people. Attachment, then, is the process that enslaves desire and creates the state of addiction.[5]

Thus, addiction (and attachment) represent the hidden you, the false self, the fig-leaf-covered person who lives in fear and shame, apart from union with God. This you — your false self — is not a *bad* self. It's simply you living apart from your deepest core, in union with God. This is the definition of sin: alienation from God, which includes alienation from your true self in union with God. And this state of alienation is what produces all that is bad and evil and damaging to you and to those you love.

And it's the self that cannot be known by God and by others because it is a mirage, a ruse. This is why I often say that I believe only one percent of what an addict tells me. So possessed by his alien self, the addict is unable to see what is healthy and what is unhealthy. And though he may seem in complete control, and convince you of it, his control is paper-thin, ready to tear and break at any moment.

However, because I believe that the addict is defined not by his addiction but by his deepest identity in God, I hope that if I stand alongside him, listening and even speaking directly to his better self, he might begin to hear the whisper of God, the welcome of the Father to the prodigal, the promise of forgiveness and a blessing. Knowing this reality is crucial to standing in the mess of an addict's life.

The Addict as Both Wounded and Wounding

The next reality I want you to see is that the addict is both someone who is wounded and someone who is also wounding others in the process. I struggle with the endless debates among different camps that argue about whether or not some addictions are a disease or a choice. Scripture seems to hold both realities in tension — that we both inherit the sins of the fathers (Deut. 5:9) and bear responsibility for our own sins (Deut. 24:16). There is always a complicated set of variables involved — environment, parenting, socio-economic factors, medical history, even the genetic roll-of-the-dice.

I know a family with three children. The first child is in law school, a well-adjusted, healthy individual who seems to excel at everything. The second has been in and out of boarding school, addiction recovery programs, and other corrective systems. The third child is a sweet young girl, still in high school, having had to navigate the chaos that her middle brother created, often crying herself to sleep. So, who's to blame? Who's to say that her oldest brother isn't a self-righteous prig who has driven the others to futility and frustration (Luke 15:28-29)? Who's to say that the father's busy work life and absence at ball games and music concerts isn't a precipitating factor? Did the birth of the sister take attention away from her troubled brother? And what about the mother's history of anxiety issues, leading her to a lifetime of using prescription medications that include Valium, Xanax, and Prozac? Or what about the troubled brother's early "best friend," who gave him his first drink? Who's to blame?

Do you see the level of complexity?

For this reason, in my approach I take two realities very seriously. First, the addict brings a host of issues to bear which he may not be responsible for. The "beautiful complexity" I spoke of in Chapter 2 is one that may include a unique composition of genetic traits which set him up for a lifetime of addiction and abuse. I think of the courageous biographical account of William Cope Moyers, son of the well-known political consultant and television personality Bill Moyers, a man who came from a solid family but seemed to bear the signs of a troubled personality from a very early age. Cope's personal account in his biography, *Broken,* doesn't assign blame, but simply tells his story. And what is clear is that Cope simply came out of his mother's womb with a very different temperament than his siblings. Though they were raised in the same home, it was clear that Cope was hardwired for trouble.[6]

And yet, at the same time, all of us are decision-makers. We make choices, choices which we must take responsibility for. Yes, we may have experienced significant wounding, whether through our genetics or through abuse. We may have inherited generations of addiction. Still, our choices are our choices. It is a uniquely human reality that we are not mindless automatons, or toys which are wound up and sent on our way. We are responsible agents. One of my addict clients said something very courageous in this regard some time ago: "It's true that I've been hurt, but let's face it — I've done my part to sabotage every healthy relationship I've ever been in." That kind of honesty goes a long way in the healing process.

This reality has been recognized among business leaders, not only psychologists and pastors. In *Deep Change,* which presents new paradigms for leadership in the corporate world, Robert Quinn writes,

> When we see the need for deep change, we usually see it as something that needs to take place in someone else. In our roles of authority, such as parent, teacher, or boss, we are particularly quick to direct others to change. Such directives often fail, and we respond to the resistance by increasing our efforts. The power struggle that follows seldom results in change or brings about excellence. One of the most important insights about the need to bring about deep change in others has to do with where deep change actually starts.[7]

Quinn rightly sees that deep change begins when we face ourselves, taking responsibility for our own lives.

What I have seen for many years is that addicts tend to come from families where some form of addiction has been experienced. I've known many sex addicts who later discover that Dad, Grandpa, and others have struggled with pornography and masturbation. I've counseled many young women with eating disorders whose mothers were addicted in one way or another, whether to plastic surgery or the perfectly ordered home. And yet, while I empathize with and understand the deep level of complexity involved in systemic and even generational addictive sin, each addict is responsible for his or her recovery. And, thanks to the wisdom of Christian tradition, as well as Alcoholics Anonymous and its embedded Christian spirituality, many addicts are taking that courageous journey — a journey which requires radical honesty and self-awareness, a profound ownership of one's issues and the impact of those issues on others, and the bold move of making amends.

A Threefold Strategy

When confronted with a situation where addiction may be an issue, how do you proceed? Is there a decision-making process to assess the problem and the level of need?

For some time, I've been employing a threefold approach to helping, whether I'm helping an addict or counseling someone with a very different set of issues. The threefold model is really quite simple. It approaches problems with the recognition that we are complicated creatures who experience change on multiple levels. I'll call these levels the functional, the systemic, and the transformational.[8] And the addict's community — church, friends, family, co-workers, managers, family therapist, and family doctor — all play a role in each.

In my estimation, this threefold process takes into account the main ways in which psychologists and theologians tend to conceptualize problems. At the functional level, the approach is short-term and strategic, addressing the very pressing behavioral issues. At the systemic level, the approach probes further, addressing the roots of the issue, including one's past and current family system.[9] Finally, at the transformational level, the approach goes beyond behavioral change and personal analysis in order to ask, "Where is God in this?" This approach sees the deepest healing in (re)union with God. These, of course, are not necessarily linear stages, but ways of approaching caring for the addict.

Let's look at all three by using the examples of four imaginary addicts, the kind of people we all may know:

Jeff is a sex addict. A successful businessman, he's been caught in multiple affairs, and struggles regularly with Internet pornography.

Trish self-mutilates. Her boyfriend noticed that she was cutting herself, while hiding her wounds from her parents and others with long-sleeved clothing.

Roy is an alcoholic. He drinks socially after work until his friends leave. Then he often finds the nearest liquor store and buys enough vodka to cover the remainder of the evening, and the following afternoon.

Elaine is an anorexic. She's a high-achieving young leader who exercises frequently and looks very fit, but who regularly battles exhaustion and loneliness.

Addressing the Functional Level

When you discover that Jeff, Trish, Roy, and Elaine are battling addiction of one kind or another, your first task is to assess the situation. No matter what role you play — pastor, manager, family member — you have certain questions to ask, certain decisions to make. You need to assess the seriousness of the situation. This means asking very specific questions: How often are Jeff and Trish acting out, and in what contexts? How much is Roy drinking? How is Elaine's anorexia playing out (not eating, over-exercising, and so on)? Are there precipitating triggers or factors (loneliness, depression, anxiety, a fight with a spouse, an issue at work, spiritual dryness, etc.)? Has suicide been considered, and is there a plan? How are personal and work contexts being affected? How is family being affected? (For example, is Roy driving while intoxicated, perhaps even with his children in the car?)

Keep in mind, however, that with each "revelation" of the addict's behavior, his/her shame, fear of judgment, or fear of consequences (losing a job or a marriage) may increase. Thus, you need to proceed with a great deal of care and compassion, developing trust and cultivating a sense of safety. A safe community of friends and specialists is critical for the addict.

When you're assessing, you're looking for two main things — the seriousness of the addiction, and the addict's level of self-awareness or ownership of his problem.

First, by asking good, specific questions, you assess how serious the addiction might be.[10] All addictions exist on a continuum. Many addicts are quite adept at living with the addictive behavior, and can easily convince us that they're just fine. But in many cases, they're barely holding life together, and oftentimes both their psychological and their physical health are suffering. When the level of seriousness is determined, the decision-making process then turns to functional needs.

Second, you need to determine the addict's level of ownership of his/her issues, as well as his/her willingness to feel and see how the addiction is impacting others. Because addiction is profoundly narcissistic, addicts struggle to empathize with the pain they are inflicting on others, let alone themselves. Prone to controlling their feelings as well as those around them, addicts resist feeling powerless, or accepting the significance of the pain others face.

As professor and therapist Sharon Hersh writes, "Addiction . . . is giving my heart and soul over to something that I believe will ease my pain and provide an outlet for my fury at being out of control in a world that hurts me, scares me, or leaves me alone."[11] While maintaining control, some addicts may be in complete denial that their significant others know, or that their work performance is being impacted, or that their health is at risk.

With an assessment of both the seriousness of the addiction and the addict's level of personal ownership and responsibility, you can piece together a strategy to help. These steps will differ for each addict — such as Jeff, Trish, Roy, and Elaine — for a variety of reasons. But in each case, certain behavioral choices will be suggested, including who will know, who the care team will be, what boundaries need to be set in order to rein in the behavior, and what level of re-assessment will be needed over the coming weeks and months.

Let's look at two imaginary scenarios involving Elaine and Jeff.

Elaine's gaunt appearance was an initial sign to coworkers and family that something might be wrong. Sometimes we fear "intruding" or asking an inappropriate question, but with compassion and care Elaine's boss expressed concern for her health. Because this leader was concerned not only with her employee's performance but with the "whole" person, she conveyed her concerns in a way that pledged confidentiality and commitment. During this functional stage, the doctor determined that Elaine's health was at great risk, because she was very underweight and beginning to show key symptoms, including lanugo — downy hair that covers the entire body to keep it warm in the absence of fat. Elaine's early plan required a brief hospitalization, and her long-term plan would include regular therapy and medical assessment. Her manager, along with a strong and wise human resources team, carefully handled her situation with confidentiality and grace, and Elaine was back to work in two weeks while engaging in a regular process of therapy (systemic) and whole health care.

Jeff, on the other hand, resisted the initial attempts of friends to show him care and help him take his sexual addiction and extra-marital affairs seriously. As a result, the functional stage bypassed some of the normal initial interventions for a sex addict, including a professional assessment by a therapist, some behavioral boundaries (involving Internet use, work trips, credit-card use, and so on), and short-term marital counseling to address where he lives, how he interacts with his kids about the issues, and other key factors. Instead, Jeff's community of friends and his pastor had to raise the stakes. With great grief, his wife asked him to leave their home, and his closest friends staged an intervention. At times, a functional approach requires some tough love in order to help get the addict to the point of owning his issues.

ADDRESSING THE SYSTEMIC LEVEL

It usually takes some significant functional progress for the deeper, systemic work to take place with an addict. It is difficult to begin to address the addict's family dynamics, to facilitate healing conversations, or to explore weighty family-of-origin issues if the addict's life is in chaos. Therefore, before the systemic level can be addressed, an assessment must be done, and the initial plan to stabilize the person must begin taking effect.

I know this well, because as a clinician I often have addicts referred to me who are steeped in their addiction and mired in chaos and drama. A family member will say, "Please help him — I think this all goes back to his issues with his father!" to which I'll respond, "Maybe, but we're not at all ready for that conversation yet." Systemic work will be successful only when the addict has achieved some sobriety, and is ready and stable enough to do the more difficult internal and interpersonal work.

There are two main aspects to systemic work — internal and interpersonal. Internal work often involves individual therapy and looks at the addict's life, significant family relationships, and other key elements. Interpersonal work deals with the addict's style of relating and current relationships, including those with family, co-workers, friends, and so on. The two often happen simultaneously.

Let's imagine that I, as a pastor, bring together Roy, an alcoholic, and his wife and three children, ages ten, thirteen, and fifteen. This can happen because Roy has accepted the seriousness of his addiction and has cooperated with a functional plan which includes cutting out all alcoholic beverages, attending AA meetings, and getting therapy. Having gained some distance and clarity, Roy is now able to hear how his drinking has impacted his family. Roy weeps and apologizes for hiding his drinking, and even endangering himself and his children when he drove while intoxicated. He listens carefully to his family as each of them shares how his drinking has personally impacted them. And a shattered trust is gradually re-built. Roy's interpersonal relationships can begin to heal.

At the same time, Roy sees a therapist, and their work is clear: beginning to tackle Roy's internal, family-of-origin issues. His father, uncles, and grandfather were all very functional alcoholics, much like Roy, and Roy's own pain of seeing his father leave for the bar each evening and return drunk and emotionally cut-off was uncovered and grieved. In time, Roy begins to see that his drinking was just a symptom of a deeper issue. What preceded his behavior was a feeling of profound loneliness, an ache that had been with him for many years. Drink filled the void — in fact, it became a friend. With alcohol, he could move past his sense of loneliness and even abandonment and feel empowered, numbed to his heartache. Though in his sobriety he once again feels the sting of emptiness within, he is courageously holding out hope for a more lasting union.

ADDRESSING THE TRANSFORMATIONAL LEVEL

"A more lasting union." I use this phrase quite intentionally because I do believe all real wholeness, healing, and transformation occur in union with God, as the false self is shed, as attachments are released, and as the deepest, truest self surrenders in dependence on God. This would be the necessary process for Roy. Not only would he need to make functional, behavioral shifts and tackle systemic issues, but in relinquishing his substitute love — alcohol — he would be transformed, open to a new depth of love in God.

This is the "divine therapy," as Father Thomas Keating calls it. Keating writes,

> The spiritual journey is not a career or success story. It is a series of humiliations of the false self that become more and more profound. These make room inside us for the Holy Spirit to come in and heal. What prevents us from being available to God is gradually evacuated. We keep getting closer and closer to our center. Every now and then God lifts a corner of the veil and enters into our awareness through various channels, as if to say, "Here I am. Where are you? Come and join me."[12]

Where are you? These are the words God called as he searched for the hidden Adam and Eve. And this is the heart of every good therapist, parent, pastor, or friend dealing with an addict. It is the search for the true self.

As much as functional strategies are vital and systemic awareness (and the consequent grieving and other experiences) is crucial, healing that goes to the core is healing that is done in union with God. And the addict, perhaps more than anyone else, is primed for this encounter. As Alcoholics Anonymous has shown with such sterling clarity, an addict's healing journey begins with the recognition that she is powerless, unable to save herself, completely at the mercy of a compassionate God. Indeed, this is where Jesus begins his teaching too, gathering his young, cocky disciples on a hill and saying, "Blessed are the poor in spirit, for theirs is the Kingdom." The poor are the *ptochoi,* those who have come to the end of themselves, those who've hit rock bottom. And, it's not just addicts who need this. We all need such grace.

I wish this transformative process was easy, and I certainly wish I could describe a process by which we could all be very painlessly released from our burdens. I've spent years praying for some people mired in addiction. And I've been hurt in very personal ways by addicts who've continued on their self-destructive journeys, at great cost to me and to others. But I've also seen remarkable, unpredictable transformation.

Let's consider transformation for Trish, the young woman who cuts herself. After years of therapy for a variety of issues, including cutting herself, Trish was able to gain some measure of functional control, employing a variety of strategies. She'd call others when she was triggered to cut. She went to a support group, saw a therapist, and tried to create a healthy life for herself to the extent she could control it. She was also able to go beyond this to the systemic, identifying the pain in her life which created the ugly internal reality of wanting to hurt herself. She'd spent years grieving sexual abuse. And she rightly saw that cutting was her way of feeling pain in a way she could manage and control. And yet, she still cut.

But it was on a Good Friday when a deeper transformation and healing began. Trish was hiding the scars of yet another episode of cutting when she came to church that night. As she walked into the sanctuary, she was immediately struck by a series of vivid images which were scrolling on the screen in the front, accompanied by the haunting music of Palestrina's "Lamentations of Jeremiah." And as she sat, awed by images of Christ bloodied and wounded on the cross, she glanced down at Isaiah 53:5 on the cover of her worship program:

> The punishment that brought us peace was on him, and by his wounds we are healed.

Though she'd heard the message of Good Friday preached many times, it was that evening that a God who had seemed far off when she was being sexually abused now seemed as close as her most intimate friend — even closer. This God dwelled in her. And because her life was somehow mysteriously "hidden in Christ" (Col. 3:3), she had no need to continue to wound herself. Prior to this night, her tears were tears of self-pity. On this Good Friday, her tears were a release, a surrender, as a profound joy filled places in her that had ached for two decades.

This is transformation, and it's an ongoing process in the life of each of us.

The Gift of Addiction

Addicts who've experienced something of what Trish experienced will tell you that addiction was and is a gift. I know addicts long sober who still go to regular meetings because of the grace and honesty they experience there, and because it presents the opportunity to support others in the struggle. I also know some who feel as if they wear the scarlet letter in their church or workplace, experiencing the judgmental eye of a pastor, or the gracelessness of a self-righteous co-worker. And yet, these men and women also view their addiction as a gift which has led to new intimacy with God, and new grace for others.

Over the years I've had pastors and leaders tell me that those who have struggled with addiction and experienced significant recovery and transformation are the most humble, hard-working, and honest people they know. I've witnessed the same. But I've also seen a strange phenomenon — men and women who might not necessarily be called "addicts" seeing their own enslavements and recognizing similar addictive patterns. Reputation, power, financial security, and many other subtle attachments can bind us, depleting our energy, hurting our relationships, and even blocking deeper intimacy with God. And so, in one sense, we're all on the journey to recovery.

The vision we have for ourselves and for others, however, is not one of mere sobriety or behavioral change. The vision is for transformation. I once had an experienced therapist tell me that the only real "cure" he'd ever seen for addiction was a deeper experience of union with God. The addict's hunger and thirst are satisfied only in this union and communion, which has led many of them to find great joy in the Christian sacrament of the Eucharist, in contemplative prayer, or in long periods of silence and solitude.

While I wouldn't wish addiction on my daughters, let alone anyone I know, what I do know is that I pray for transformation — for my daughters, for my wife, for myself, and for those I lead. And I know this process very necessarily involves the kind of humiliation that leads to humility, brokenness that leads to surrender and dependence on God. In God's mysterious economy of things, the addict may stand most able to display transformation.

loving the fool:
when relationships turn ugly

People with a big head are headed for a fall, preten-
tious egos brought down a peg. It's GOD alone at
front-and-center.

ISAIAH 2:11 *(THE MESSAGE)*

Bold love is courageously setting aside our personal
agenda to move humbly into the world of others with
their well-being in view, willing to risk further pain in
our souls, in order to be an aroma of life to some and the
aroma of death to others.

DAN ALLENDER

Whoever corrects a mocker invites insults;
whoever rebukes the wicked incurs abuse.
Do not rebuke mockers or they will hate you;
rebuke the wise and they will love you.

PROVERBS 9:7-8

THE DIFFICULT PEOPLE we deal with each day may not struggle with personality disorders or addiction. Some of them are simply foolish; others are profoundly sinister. This brings the hard work of loving difficult people to an entirely different level, one that requires another set of tools. Sometimes it's a trusted friend or staff member who acts like someone entirely different than you've come to know, betraying your trust and behaving in ways that call you to question your own judgment. On other occasions, you may be faced with twisted and distorted accusations or threats that reveal the wiles of a cruel, calculating, and cunning foe.

As we've recognized, we're all far more complex than we know. You might be thinking of a dark secret hidden in the long, invisible bag you drag behind you. You may even be a bit frightened by your own thoughts and actions at times. Truth be told, we've all deceived ourselves and others.

There is a difference, however. Your honest awareness of secret motives and troubling relational styles shows that you've taken an aggressive posture in rooting out all that might rot your heart and ruin your relationships. Truly foolish or sinister souls are typically quite unaware of their own motives and undaunted by the results of their actions.

In this chapter, we'll explore the rugged and sometimes dangerous road of loving the fool, who blithely acts in foolish or sinful ways with little or no understanding of where these actions come from in himself or what their consequences are for others. Unable or unwilling to live from the deeper truth of who he is in Christ, he may be so trapped in his false self that it's the only reality he knows. To those who confront him with the truth, he might say what the unfaithful ambassadors of King Hezekiah said long ago when challenged with their foolish ways: "Give us no more visions of what is right! Tell us pleasant things, prophesy illusions" (Isa. 30:10). The Bible calls this person a "fool," one who cannot see or

will not see his folly for what it is, and thus cannot own or acknowledge the damage done to those in the relational debris left behind.

Foolishness in Context

Scripture regularly places wisdom and folly in juxtaposition. However, we only have to take a good look at ourselves to recognize
that they are not mutually exclusive categories. We're a mixture
of both wisdom and foolishness — all of us. This is why Scripture
talks about the way of wisdom and the way of foolishness. It's not
so much about ontology, our essential nature; it's more about ge-
ography — where we've been and where we're going. Are we open
to the truth of who we are, or are we entrenched and unwilling to
see? Wisdom, after all, is about seeing.

In one of my favorite books, *Bold Love,* Dan Allender and Tremper Longman envision three categories of sinner: an evil person, a
fool, and a normal sinner.[1] The authors admit that these categories
are more flexible than rigid. Because we're complex, and because
so much of who we are can be hidden from sight, it's not unusual
to see the so-called normal sinner fall into a pattern of extremely
foolish, even sinister behavior. Look at yourself. Most people might
think you're a pretty decent person, and you probably are. That
is, until you're triggered by a comment your spouse makes, or an
injustice at work, or an issue that irks you. Out comes the fury,
or bitterness, or cynicism. Perhaps your kids are in your warpath.
Perhaps a friend gets the brunt of it. Worse still, when challenged,
you make excuses. You play it down. You blame others.

Several hours later, in the quiet of your soul, it hits you: *I just blew
it.* You see how blinded you were. As the false self shrinks, you're
back to being you. Maybe you even feel as if you've just re-emerged
in your own skin. You splash a bit of water on your face, and then

ask yourself, *Who was that? Why that kind of rage? Why the denial?* Yes, you've just played the fool. The difference between you and the fool is that you see the behavior for what it is, and you're willing to own it before God and others. You're back on the way of wisdom.

The way of foolishness, as I see it, progresses as follows:

The Simple Fool → The Self-Consumed Fool → The Sinister Fool

Each step along the way further entrenches a person in the blindness of folly, as they veer further off the path of wisdom.

And each step along the way animates what I call the "perils" of foolishness — arrogance, blindness, and an incapacity for empathy, all of which will be explored in greater depth as we proceed. However, let's briefly take a look at this in light of what we've been exploring in previous chapters.

As I understand the human psyche, our tendency to stuff large parts of ourselves into that invisible bag can lead someone to lead a life lived out of a finely tuned false self, arrogantly sure of the rightness of her way. Biblically, this might be called a life of folly.

While certainly not all foolish people suffer from the personality disorders we discussed in Chapter 3, foolishness is also deeply influenced by genetics, family history, neurobiology, abuse, and other factors. Though this does not absolve anyone of personal responsibility, it does invite us to offer fools greater empathy, aware of the complex set of circumstances and experiences that likely shaped their personalities.

The Simple Fool

Judy was a 68-year-old client who came to see me, her pastor, because her adult children were exasperated with her behavior.

Her daughter, Jill, and her son, Rob, came in for the first session, explaining that both of their marriages were strained because of Judy's intrusiveness, as well as her bizarre grandparenting tactics. Judy seemed nice enough, but she was somewhat oblivious as Jill and Rob recited stories of Judy's constant phone calls, her unplanned drop-ins, and her inability to keep boundaries. They told me of the many times that Judy would be babysitting or watching the grandkids overnight, but would blatantly refuse to follow the parents' guidelines. In one case, Grandma Judy cooked fish sticks for the grandchildren, ignoring little Jesse's diagnosis of celiac disease, which resulted in an emergency-room visit. When her children confronted her, Judy said, "When you were kids, you ate everything. I don't believe all this nonsense about allergies!"

Arrogance, blindness, and a lack of empathy are all characteristics of a fool. In many ways, Judy was a good woman who tirelessly gave time to her local community's food pantry and graciously made herself available to babysit the grandchildren. But she simply refused to respect the clear and understandable boundaries that most others easily recognized. She simply believed that she knew better when it came to dealing with everything from allergies to visits, and was unaware of the impact she was having on others. Rob, Jill, and their spouses had tried explaining these things to Judy, as well as writing letters and e-mails, all to no avail. Talking to her pastor was her children's final attempt to deal with years of frustration.

I spent six sessions with Judy, and we talked about many things. It became clear that she was not malicious. If anything, Judy was guilty of being ignorant. But why? Before long, we waded into the deep waters of Judy's soul. After she lost her husband, Tim, to cancer, Judy didn't grieve. Telling others she was fine, she immersed herself in the lives of others, busying herself with helping when she was really hurting inside. In time, we began to see this as her lifelong pattern. At age twelve she became her mother's "helper" when her father died, leaving behind Judy's young mother and four children. Judy became "little Mom," over-involved in the parenting and care of her siblings, and unable to enjoy her teenage years.

When the grief began to flow in tears, Judy began to awaken to her lifelong patterns. In addition, she discovered that she'd never lived as anyone other than the helper, a thought that saddened and also repulsed her. One day she shouted, "I want to learn to golf because I want to learn to golf!" It was an extraordinary relief to her children as Judy discovered a life beyond her identity as helper. And indeed, it was an extraordinary discovery for her to find that she had a Father who had longed to love her all these many years when she was too busy to receive love.

Pastor Craig Barnes writes,

> Since people are unaccustomed to exploring the mystery of their own souls, they will often work out their spiritual anxieties by attempting to rearrange something external. . . . But it doesn't matter how many changes they make to the environment around them. They will never succeed in finding peace for the angst of the soul until they attend directly to it.[2]

So-called simple fools are not averse to the pathway of wisdom; they simply do not know how to walk on it. Perhaps they've never been shown the way. Perhaps they were never apprenticed in it. Without any intention on the fool's part, the way of folly emerges as the false self, constructed to survive in a world that can be very challenging. Neural pathways are formed and endure, as our brains know no other way than this one. That's why it can be so difficult for the simple fool to discover the truth about herself.

The simple fool, more often than not, needs someone on the way of wisdom to walk gently, graciously, and non-judgmentally alongside him or her. After years of frustration, Jill and Rob were unable to get out of their own reactive selves in order to understand their mother. They were too close to her and bound up in the relational situation. And this scenario is typical. That's why it often takes someone outside the close circle of relationships to attend to the soul.

Some might argue that Judy's children should be confronted for not "honoring" their mother. She's older, after all, and not malicious, so leave her alone! Some might say that Judy should be confronted with her "sinful" disregard for her grandchildren's well-being.

Skillful and empathetic leaders, however, see the bigger picture. We cast a larger net, and patiently wait for the revealing facts to swim in. Slowly, over time, we piece together the story. With grace and care, we help people tell their story in such a way that brings enlightenment and self-understanding. In many respects, that's what preaching does. That's what pastoral care does. That's what good leadership does.

We are story-gatherers and story-tellers, and real wisdom comes in how we weave them together. We're not called to make people feel bad or guilty. We're called to lead them to an honest appraisal of themselves, which in turn leads to honesty before God and others.

So, who are the simple fools? I'm afraid there are many of us. Folly rears its ugly head in a thousand ways. I was speaking with a pastor just recently who fell back into pornography use, denying it to his wife until he was found out. This man is, in many respects, a very wise soul. But old patterns die hard. With grace and care, I pray that this man finds himself back on the path of wisdom. However, he'll need to recognize the folly of lying and covering up, and the pain that causes others.

I'm also mindful of the simple fool who may be your spouse. You married him because he was a good guy, loyal, and hard-working. But he's emotionally cut off. He falls asleep each night with a beer in one hand and a remote in the other. He loves you, but he's stuck. He needs someone who will help him make sense of his story.

The simple fool is the university professor who is brilliant, but relationally stunted. She responds to your request to talk with her about a grade with an arrogant exclamation: "I don't have time for whining students!" But in her best moments, she is engaged and inspiring.

The simple fool is the person on your leadership team who is profoundly gifted yet has little emotional intelligence. She doesn't wake up in the morning with the intention of disrupting the office and frustrating her fellow team members. She is merely blind to a pattern of relating that may eventually cost her a job.

The simple fool is the person who regularly sends you e-mail complaints, failing to see that he's acting out a script that is not about you at all, but about his disappointment with Dad.

The simple fool is a thorn in your side, but just a thorn, not a millstone around your neck. You are called to keep in mind that his or her story is bigger than what you now know. You are invited to see this person not as a problem to be solved but as a mystery to be known. Ever mindful of your own blindness, you are called to wade patiently into the murky waters of relationship, remembering that at heart the simple fool longs to be known and loved by God and others just like you. Beneath the frustrating false self is an image-bearing soul, loved by God and waiting to be known by you. Building a relationship is always costly, but it's worth the cost because it's an investment in another living soul.

The Self-Consumed Fool

Brian became head of marketing at his firm at just twenty-six years old. Charismatic and smart, he'd won over the older executives, but he hadn't fooled Christa. She knew Brian's game. As the VP who would work most closely with him, she knew he'd try to play the game on her, too. Brian saw the world as a competition, and he'd do what it took to win the game. Success was paramount for him, and Christa feared that Brian's tactics were not known to the Board and the CEO, and was sure they would not be approved. In a pre-emptive strike, however, Brian forwarded portions of several e-mails that Christa had written which, framed appropriately, seemed to indicate that Christa had lost confidence in the Board's ability to make good decisions, and questioned the CEO's judgment. Gleefully, Brian sent a one-word e-mail to Christa: *Gotcha.*

Arrogance. Blindness. A lack of empathy. Brian embodies all of these. What Christa doesn't know, however, is that Brian is my client. As his therapist, I've heard about her, and I feel for her. Brian's manipulative ways have put her role and future in jeopardy. I'm quite sure that she's second-guessing her writing of e-mails that in any way call her superiors into question. And I'm certain that she's exasperated, perhaps ready to sabotage her position anyway just to get out of Brian's line of fire.

Brian is a fool, a self-consumed fool. He's crossed the line from ignorance to manipulation. At some level he knows what he's doing. To be sure, he doesn't know the deeper story of his soul. That's my job to illuminate. But he knows he plays games. Still, he's almost gleeful as he learns about himself. "You're damn right, Chuck," he says. "I'll do anything to make it to the top." His self-awareness has not yet led to humility.

Brian is a narcissist. While the label may be useful in discerning Brian's behavior, it can also get in the way if it deflects me from working with him in the framework of love. But Brian is tough to love. I despise his narcissistic behavior and the way it impacts the people in his life. However, by this point in therapy, I'm actually beginning to like the Brian I see beneath the façade. He presents himself as a hotshot, but I know better. In truth, he's an insecure little boy. His controlling and perfectionistic father had him playing every sport when he was growing up, so life did indeed become a game. Women became a game too, as Dad cheated on Mom, and Brian was made to clean up the collateral damage so that Mom wouldn't find out. Brian started his training in marketing for his father at age six. The goal was clear. Life's purpose was to win.

What I know as Brian's therapist — but Christa doesn't know — is that he has fallen for her. Insecure to the core, he doesn't know how to access and share his real feelings, so love becomes sport as well. He sees his behavior as flirtation, while Christa sees it as humiliation. When I share this with Brian, he can't see it. "Ahh, she loves it, Chuck. You've been married too long. You don't have a clue about women." That's what he says, but I can see in his face that he does care, even if it's just a little bit. Brian lacks empathy, but his heart is not dead. In his more vulnerable moments, he is able to tap into a deeper core within, but any sense of threat brings him back to his fierce, competitive, false self. He has endured too much pain to be willing to fully let down his guard.

I share both perspectives on this story — mine and Christa's — because I get to see beneath the surface of Brian's self-consumed foolishness. And what I know to be true is that Brian is a broken, insecure little boy who is stuck in his early teens emotionally, still playing his games, still trying to win. The key for Christa, and for others who relate to fools like Brian, is to see this too — to see beyond the harsh exterior into the softer, more vulnerable interior. When they do, they'll stop playing the fool's game — but they need to be prepared to fight a different kind of battle.

Allender and Longman call tangling with a person like this "guerrilla warfare" because engaging a fool like Brian requires subtlety and the element of surprise.[3] Brian will always strive to win his game. But love is different. It's not a game. It is cruciform, patterned after the love of Christ. It doesn't fight to win; it fights to love. You may not win this battle, but it's the only thing worth fighting for.

So, how do you and I love this fool? I have some general rules when working with the self-consumed fool. While they may not fit every situation, they do serve as a general framework for loving difficult people like Brian.

First, assess yourself. To deal with someone like Brian, you'll need a firm sense of your core identity in God, as loved and secure beyond anything that could happen to you. A strong, stable identity allows you to relate to a self-consumed fool from a posture of security rather than reactivity. Because a self-consumed fool looks for weakness and preys on it, your strength and solidity will allow you to move toward him in a loving yet firm way. And when your core identity is solid, nothing the fool can do will ultimately hurt you.

While none of us would likely say we have a perfectly firm core identity in Christ, there are some of us who are simply not prepared to engage this kind of fool because of a lack of a stable, strong, and secure self. If you are not secure in your own identity, and if you do not have a community around you reminding you of who you are, your responses to the self-consumed fool will tend to be reactive, volatile, and self-protective. You'll need to get help from your pastor, a therapist, or a community that can nurse you back to health, to a point that you're able to engage once more.

Second, I counsel people to stop playing the fool's game, whatever his manipulative game might be. Every fool lives according to a certain unhealthy pattern which sucks others into its vortex. You must identify the pattern and do what you can to live outside of it and beyond it, even if it means moving out, breaking up, or asking a boss or a manager to have a desk or a seating arrangement changed at work.

Now, refusing to play the fool's game can evoke rage in the fool.

If you're married to an abusive fool, stopping the game may feel dangerous. At this point, you'll need the help of a wise therapist and a community, if not the authorities. To keep your resolve, remember that in general, playing the game doesn't work. You must realize that you're caught in a battle you can't win. Christa found herself so intimidated by Brian that she stopped talking to him directly and began e-mailing him, still taking him on but unwittingly providing him with fodder for his own attack.

Third, but closely related to the previous point: I encourage setting clear boundaries. Because a fool lacks self-awareness, he will continue to grab more power. To a self-consumed fool, setting boundaries can be seen as yet another part of the game, and he will try to find a way around them. Once again, having a secure, stable identity allows you to remain anchored when the fool tries repeatedly to win the game. A clear sense of what you will and won't permit protects you, and also puts the fool on notice. If he crosses a boundary, a greater distancing will likely need to occur. In a marriage, separation may be required. In other cases, discipline or termination may need to occur. In the sticky situation in which Christa finds herself, she'll need to decide if she's willing to work through this dysfunctional work relationship, or if she's going to look for another position.

Fourth, speak to both "selves" of the fool — the false self and the true, core self. One of my clients said to her self-consumed, foolish husband, "I love the you that emerges when you let down your guard, but I cannot and will not interact with the side of you that rages and controls." You stay engaged with a fool at some level because of the belief that something more exists beneath the false self. As Frederick Buechner reminded us earlier, "Life batters and shapes us in all sorts of ways before it's done, but those original selves which we were born with . . still echo with the holiness of their origin."[4] It's hard to see this core holiness beneath the angry, controlling, raging, and manipulating foolish self. But remember that speaking to both parts of a person acknowledges both the reality that some things cannot be tolerated and the hope that there is a true self that can be awakened and called out.

Fifth, because loving a fool requires a kind of guerrilla warfare, subtlety and surprise are key. With a self-consumed fool, you don't fight offensively and directly. Perhaps this is why St. Paul calls upon the use of "spiritual weapons" in Ephesians 6. A cruciform, loving approach to a fool requires not reactivity and volatility, but spiritual wisdom and weaponry. This, of course, is not an invitation to let an abuser get away with abusing you.[5] It does, however, set you on a trajectory of love, with the hope of forgiveness and reconciliation unless it proves impossible.

This approach can be seen in the prophet Nathan's confrontation of King David (read 2 Samuel 12). Nathan uses a parable to illuminate David's sin. Jesus often uses parables in the same way in the Gospels. Jesus knew what psychologists and neuroscientists have discovered today — that the logical left brain will always keep us in the mode of control and self-deception, but that the storied right side of the brain is more open to hear the truth. The psychologist Milton Erickson knew this, and he made an art of telling stories that often surprised and jolted his patients into seeing their own issues.[6]

During a session with Brian, I asked if I could get his advice on another client of mine. Narcissists love being experts, and Brian readily complied, sitting up straight and listening intently. Here's what I said:

This father loves his daughter a lot. But he doesn't know how to show her or tell her. Recently, he's taken to slapping her in the face — not very hard, but enough to hurt. He laughs, and she begins to cry. He claims to be trying to get her attention, to get a reaction, to get her to engage . . . but she's obviously not seeing it that way. . . .

At this point in the story, Brian jumped in, enraged at the father. He said to me, "How the hell does he think he can do that to his own daughter? That's stupid. It's ridiculous." I responded, "Think about it, though. You've got a funny way of showing Christa you care for her." Brian's long silence told me that the story was chiseling away at his defenses. More often than not, subtlety and surprise can get you further than direct confrontation.

Finally, love may require you to establish significant consequences for the fool who doesn't find his way to the path of wisdom. Love does not mean staying with someone who continues to abuse. Love does not mean offering endless grace to a master manipulator. Love is neither passive nor reactive. Love acts lovingly. And that may mean termination, separation and/or divorce, church discipline, or whatever act of disconnection marks the final act of love. The word "discipline" has the same root as "discipleship," and that discipleship often requires discipline.

Whenever we establish consequences, we must check our hearts. If consequences are merely punitive, then we've missed the point. With any ending, whether it's a divorce, a termination, or even an excommunication, there may be some relief that the long, painful journey has come to an end, but there is no joy in this. As Allender and Longman write, "Bold love is courageously setting aside our personal agenda to move humbly into the world of others with their well-being in view, willing to risk further pain in our souls, in order to be an aroma of life to some and the aroma of death to others."[7] And the aroma of death, for the sake of love, is always a grief.

The Sinister Fool

In my early years as a therapist, I encountered a man whose Christian reputation seemed impeccable, but who scared the daylights out of my co-therapist and me. He seemed to prey on everyone's insecurities. He'd quote the Bible with razor-sharp acuity, yet twist its message to undermine and humiliate. After a session in which I confronted a particularly aggressive outburst from him, he e-mailed me with some of the most rationally clear but relationally twisted and condescending words I'd ever heard. He proceeded to verbally undress me in a methodical way, so much so that my own naked shame convinced me that I'd failed as a therapist. That is, until my supervisor read his e-mail aloud to me, and I could listen to what was really going on.

With pastoral compassion and patience, she reminded me — her shaken and somewhat naïve supervisee — of the story of Jesus' temptation. She reminded me that Satan quotes the Bible better than most theologians. And with a calm and reasoned voice, she told me something I'd never forget: "Chuck, you were just assaulted by an evil man."

Much of what I've said about the self-consumed fool applies to the sinister fool, but there's a crucial difference. At some level, sinister fools have been cut off, in a tragic way, from their own deepest core in God. Arrogance constitutes their being. Blindness is pervasive. Empathy has become incapacitated.

It is well-known that Adolf Hitler was abused as a child. George Victor argues that Hitler's father would beat him so often that young Adolf determined not to react anymore, willingly and even somewhat nobly (in his own estimation) taking the physical abuse. Adolf also determined not to hate his father. He would eventually grow into adulthood, wearing a uniform as his father did, carrying a whip, and mercilessly abusing hundreds of thousands. If asked about his father, he'd declare undying love and admiration. The psychic split was complete. His rage would find a scapegoat.[8]

In July of 2012, a young doctoral student entered a movie theater in Aurora, Colorado, during the showing of the newest Batman film, and fired off hundreds of rounds, killing more than a dozen people. He called himself "The Joker," a now infamous Batman series character. Why would he do this? Though an image-bearer of God, he too has experienced a pathological and tragic rupture at a core level, rendering him a sociopath.[9] Stories now appear all over the Internet, attempting to make sense of a seemingly bright and stable young man's brutal turn.

When I was teaching about this one day, a student asked, "Aren't we all just a bit sinister?" Truth be told, I do think most people I talk with will tell the story of frying a caterpillar in the microwave, or gleefully destroying a colony of ants, or worse, hurting a friend in a way that still stings with grief and regret. It is because we know our own hearts that we simultaneously express outrage and pity at a sinister fool. However, we cannot bargain with someone who is sinister.

The Bible-quoting man who preys on everyone's insecurities is not beyond the love of Christ, but his sinister ways cannot allow for any bargaining. If asked how I tell the difference between a sinister fool and a self-consumed fool, I'd have to say, "I just know." I suspect you do, too. The self-consumed fool shows occasional vulnerability. The sinister fool is impervious, shut tight, and pathologically incapable of vulnerability or self-awareness.

An interesting example of the contrast between the two types might be Peter and Judas. It's plausible to see Peter as a self-consumed fool, at least for a time, while Judas was clearly sinister.

Peter continually probed his status with Jesus, constantly asserting himself as the leader. A zealot, he knew how to win an argument. At times, he'd question Jesus to his face. At other times, he'd whisper to a friend. Lacking self-awareness, he promised integrity and faithfulness only to deliver lies and betrayal when he was threatened. He denied he knew Jesus. And yet, this man — Peter — emerged as a key leader in the early church, a saint who wrote inspired Scripture and whose obedience in death contrasts sharply with the duplicity of the man who once denied Jesus.

Judas, on the other hand, often remained behind the scenes. Filled with anger and resentment, he schemed to destroy Jesus. Not bold enough to spar publicly with Jesus like his friend Peter, he remained quiet — the nice guy, the religious guy, the one who attended all the church services and kept up his pledge. Yet, in the end, Judas betrayed the Lord, even when he understood that Jesus knew what was in his heart.

Peter will fight you, challenge you, and frustrate you. But Judas will subtly and covertly undermine you. Peter played the part of the self-consumed fool. Self-awareness returned as he heard the cock crow, and he went out and wept. His love for Jesus stood firm as he remained with the disciples through the awful and wonderful days to come. Jesus finally confronted him with a searing, thrice-asked question: "Do you love me?" Upon Peter's heartfelt response, "You know that I love you," Jesus reinstated him to leadership, saying, "Feed my sheep" (John 21:15-17).

Judas, on the other hand, the sinister fool, remained a crafty and cunning foe. Jesus, while accepting the betraying kiss, understood his evil heart. "What you are about to do," he told Judas at the Last Supper, "do quickly" (John 13:27). And while Peter ended up professing his love, Judas was incapable of self-understanding to the end, giving in to suicidal despair (Matt. 27:1-5).

I have no doubt that God's grace is big enough to embrace a Judas. That Jesus included Judas at his Last Supper is a remarkable testament to that grace. Yet the practical, everyday wisdom of the apostle Paul reminds us that there comes a time to cut ourselves off from the sinister fool (1 Cor. 5:13). While the steps elaborated in the previous section may apply during a process of discernment in these circumstances, it will become clear in time that the sinister fool is operating at an entirely different level — arrogant, blind, and completely incapable of empathy. Your job is to protect others from this person, and to pray that somehow God's grace can break the death grip of evil on his soul.[10]

Cruciform Love

As Christians, our pattern for loving others comes from the cruciform, self-giving love of Jesus. This is not a love that allows evil to trample over us, nor a love that passively accepts it. The self-giving love of Jesus is active, though not reactive. It dies a thousand deaths for the sake of the other. It calls injustice and abuse what they are, but it doesn't live enslaved by the need to get a payback. It sees the big picture, knowing that redemption is a long, slow road.

Cruciform love places us on the way of wisdom — a way of greater humility, dependence, and honesty. On this, I'm reminded of the divergent paths taken by the very foolish, yet remarkably resilient, writer of the book of Ecclesiastes. If you recall, the foolish journey he took led him to look for happiness in a variety of dead-end places — in knowledge, riches, wives, reputation, even religion. The repeated refrain captures the futility of his folly-filled journey — "Meaningless, meaningless." And he'd go on to confess that attempting to find life in these dead-end places was like "chasing after the wind" (Eccles. 2:11). His love was not cruciform, but self-consumed. His was the path of folly, a path that rejected the "fear of the Lord."

> *Now all has been heard;*
> *here is the conclusion of the matter:*
> *Fear God and keep his commandments,*
> *for this is the duty of all mankind.* (Eccles. 12:13)

However, as ominous as this ending sounds to our contemporary ears, it is not a call to anxiety in the face of a dreadful God. Rather, it's an invitation to relinquish control, to see that we're all crisscrossing the paths of wisdom and folly throughout our lives.[11] The fear of the Lord, it seems, is humility before God. And that's a lesson that takes a lifetime to learn.

And it's a lesson we all need to learn. I was speaking to a successful church-planter and pastor the other day who said, "I'm not sure that successful church planters like myself aren't all a bit narcissistic." With a mixture of laughter and shame, he went on to say, "I've run over a few people in my day." I know few successful leaders who wouldn't empathize.

The problem comes if we close our book after this chapter, saying, "Thank God I'm not a fool" (Luke 18:11). Wisdom will not allow that, however. And if there is even a bit of a whisper within your spirit that says, "There might be some foolishness in me," you've joined the writer of Ecclesiastes, among many saintly others, on this roller coaster of a Christian journey. May wisdom be yours.

Part 3

DEALING WITH OURSELVES:
THE BEST HELP WE CAN GIVE ANOTHER

growing through pain: the gift of the dark

The dark night is a key part of God's missional purpose in the world.

DANIEL SCHROCK

The journey has to feel like night because it leads to the unknown. If Christianity meant mere maintenance, then bewilderment or darkness would spell disaster. But . . . darkness is a condition of the Christian life.

IAIN MATTHEW

In embarking on the journey, we must leave the world of certainty. We must courageously journey to a strange place where there are a lot of risks and much is at stake, a place where there are new problems that require us to think in new ways.

ROBERT QUINN

I hurt myself today
To see if I still feel
I focus on the pain

The only thing that's real
The needle tears a hole
The old familiar sting
Try to kill it all away
But I remember everything.

"HURT" BY THE BAND NINE INCH NAILS

A LONE AND VERY, very cold on an Iowa winter night in 1989, I saw no point in living. My parents' marriage was all but over. Fourteen hundred miles away from my home on Long Island, I couldn't intervene as I typically would as the eldest son and hyper-vigilant system-caretaker of my family. The crumbling marriage was only a piece of an overall narrative that was coming apart at the seams. Once the model Christian family in other people's eyes, we were far from that now — our fragile guise could no longer endure the pain of reality. My parents' separation would only externalize what I knew to be real and true — that our happiness was an illusion, that life itself seemed like a cruel joke.

I could not believe anymore. And I could not hope anymore. These things only brought greater pain and disappointment. A friend said, "Chuck, lots of families are screwed up." But this was *my* family, and I felt that it wasn't just my *family* that was disintegrating — my entire worldview was falling apart. What I viewed to be rooted, steady, and reliable was not, and this opened up the bigger question: Could I imagine God being secure in this kind of brittle existence?

That night, I couldn't. When I was younger, I'd retreat to my bike or my Go-Kart, riding away from the craziness, but hopefully riding toward something more steady. When I was fifteen, I'd venture off on my scooter, a ride that would take me further still. And when I was able to drive, I'd head north, into upstate New York, looking for retreat among the rolling mountains and in the great falls at Niagara. But tonight I was looking for a more radical kind of retreat. Though I wasn't on a suicide drive, I no longer cared. If I died, so be it.

Turning onto Highway B40, I accelerated. It was dark. It was icy. And I was alone on the road, which wasn't unusual at this time of night on an Iowa highway. I continued to accelerate. When my '85 Olds Cutlass passed 80 MPH on its speedometer, I turned off my headlights and accelerated. But as the speedometer needle passed 100 MPH, something deep reached up from within me, and tears began — deep, convulsive tears that start in your gut and come pouring out of your eyes. In the blur of the next several minutes, I found myself curled up on the front seat of my car, now safely stopped, groaning, "It hurts so bad. . . . It hurts so bad."

Lying in the fetal position in my car late that night, I felt like a helpless baby who wanted the safety of a womb, a secure place where I could feel protected. But nothing felt secure.

Though our culture shouts its narrative of optimism and security, many of us feel anything but that. I'm reminded of this every day as I sit with people who tell me about their crumbling worlds. In fact, as a pastor, I'm called to remind them that what they think is secure — paychecks, degrees, beauty — is actually fleeting. Few want to hear this. In fact, pastors don't like to say it much anymore. But we are called to do it — and to remind people that every failure and heartbreak needs to be acknowledged and grieved. In many ways, we've been complicit with our culture in training people to be incapable of dealing with loss, with pain, with failure, with despair.

Jerry Sittser writes, "People in denial refuse to see loss for what it is, something terrible that cannot be reversed. But their unwillingness to face pain comes at a price. . . . In the end, denial leads to a greater loss."[1] And this greater loss comes with great cost, particularly to leaders. Though trained to motivate and encourage, we find ourselves lost in the midst of senseless pain. In many respects, what motivated me to write this book were the e-mails of pastors and leaders begging for some guidance amid the darker moments, something that seminaries, academic programs, and leadership schools don't teach.

In this chapter, I ask you to allow a sixteenth-century Spanish monk to be your teacher. Ironically, he was quite a leader, though he didn't intend to have the influence he did. A revolutionary in his day, he took the extraordinary risk of challenging a stagnant and graceless monastic movement, and calling for radical change.

A Monk's Vision

If St. John of the Cross were living today, I'm convinced he'd be most startled by the seemingly endless number of comforts people enjoy. St. John is known for resisting such comforts. Born into poverty in the year 1542, he lost his father at a young age and moved from place to place with his mother and brothers in order to survive. Like many in his day, he probably found the monastic life appealing because of his need for security, solidity, even safety. But it wouldn't take long for him to see the lie in that appeal.

Living during the same century that the Protestant Reformation took place, St. John, like Martin Luther and others, recognized the spiritual barrenness of the comfortable monastic life of his time. As he saw it, his brothers — the Carmelites — were using the monastic life as a kind of false security, a way of avoiding the demands of a cruciform life. More than that, St. John felt that they were missing out on love, which is the heart of the spiritual life. That life, after all, was about a fierce and passionate relationship with God for the sake of the world, something these comfortable monks knew little about. And so, St. John spoke up. And like the prophets before him, he was despised, rejected, and ultimately imprisoned.

Prison life in St. John's time was awful. His cell was cold, dark, and not much bigger than his body. He was publicly mocked and lashed regularly, all for challenging the comfortable lifestyle he saw among his brothers. However, the hardships of prison gradually peeled away the deeper layers of his own false security. Iain Matthew writes, "It was if the anaesthetic which normal life provides had worn off, his inner self had been scraped bare, and he now ached in a way he never had before for a God who was utterly beyond him."[2] Paradoxically, prison didn't harden St. John; it ignited in him a more fierce love, ultimately preparing him to lead a movement.

Escaping prison, St. John formed a new monastic order with the help of his friend and spiritual director, Teresa of Ávila. This was an order shaped by a vision that John had had in prison, a vision of a dark night of the soul which, he contended, brought more illumination, deeper love, and more focused mission to his life than he knew before. Saturated with the imagery of the biblical book Song of Songs, his vision featured God and the church in a tumultuous love affair, with times of great pain and absence giving way to spectacular reunions. Matthew writes,

> He proposes relationship with Christ as the adventure, and for him the negativity of life was part of that adventure. The journey has to feel like night because it leads to the unknown. If Christianity meant mere maintenance, then bewilderment or darkness would spell disaster. But . . . darkness is a condition of the Christian life.[3]

St. John assumed that without the darkness, you and I would be helplessly caught in illusory images of the good life. And he'd ask us this very hard question: "Are you offering the gospel or preaching an illusion?" The dark night for St. John is the cure for our arrogance, our blindness, our vacuum of empathy.

Exploring Darkness

What is the "dark night of the soul"? It sounds mysterious, even a bit spooky. Is it a bad day, a significant failure, a tragic loss, a deep depression?

Some have argued that St. John was only writing about something we identify as a mere psychological malady. Modern psychologists suspicious of religious language have interpreted phenomena such as the deep cries of pain in the Psalms and Lamentations and the biblical language of desertion and abandonment as nothing more than clinical depression.

Others see the dark night as merely an illusion. But there are some who see the dark night as the spiritual projection of an inner shadow-side that every human being has. Its language was fitting for primitive monks, but for the enlightened it is also empirically understandable and manageable.

In our contemporary world it's easy to scoff at the seemingly primitive thinking of a Spanish monk. But St. John of the Cross and St. Teresa of Ávila understood that psychological dynamics, not only spiritual dynamics, are often at play in a dark-night experience. Though they lacked modern categories and definitions, they exhibited keen psychological insight. St. John taught that melancholia, or depression, would often accompany the dark night. The experience wasn't either-or; it exhibited the interconnection of the psychological and the spiritual. In the midst of pain, confusion, despair, even feelings of abandonment, God was at work.

As pastors and leaders, we can learn from these wise souls. Consider the fragmented, dualistic thinking of the modern world.

Often psychologists see depression merely as a neurochemical problem that needs to be fixed with medication and therapy. And too often pastors spiritualize psychological maladies that may require further expertise. This divide would have been completely foreign to St. Teresa and St. John.

One lesson we learn from the ancient mystics is that dark nights are not only problems, but also opportunities. Grasping this reality moves us beyond the question "How do I fix this?" to the question "What is God saying to me in this?" In our North American context, we often view failure and struggle as jagged detours on what is supposed to be the smooth, straight road of life. This distinctly Western perspective also subtly impacts our Christian perceptions. Thus, pastors may think of depression, doubt, or distance from God as obstacles to ministry, rather than as opportunities for it. Leaders see their failures and weaknesses as obstacles to success, not wells of wisdom waiting to be tapped.

The dark night of the soul blocks our futile attempts to find God or to master the world on our own terms. Instead, it awakens us to the reality that we're not God! In my work I find that this is exactly what people want to discover. Pastors and leaders often tell me that they'd just like to learn to relax, to not be so much in control, to know God — more purely, more simply, more deeply. Pastors are exhausted. Leaders are burning out. They desire something more, but they fear losing control, losing power, losing credibility or respect. We've made the darkness an enemy. But we've got to see the darkness as a friend.

Tracing the Dark Shadow in Our Pasts

When I emerged from my '85 Olds Cutlass on that dark, cold night, I knew I needed therapy. I scheduled an appointment with our school counselor the next week. He asked me some questions and seemed to have my family pegged in about thirty minutes. He identified my mom, who courageously battled alcoholism years before my birth, as my first problem. My second problem was my dad, who worked relentlessly to provide for his family. The counselor gave me a book to read, along with a little pep talk. And off I was sent, with a bit of insight, but still a lot of pain.

Families are often a source of our later dysfunction, and lots of good clinical work revolves around systemic family issues. But in the effort to find a cause or a culprit for our difficulties, it's easy to miss the opportunity to trace the dark shadow through our pasts and into our present.

In Chapter 2, I reflected on the long, invisible bag that we all drag behind us, filled with parts of ourselves that we deem unwanted, ugly, or deficient. Though Mom and Dad may be part of that baggage, each of us has the responsibility to open our own bag, analyze its contents, and reflect on their meaning for us. Whatever shadows they cast, it's now up to us to become adults, and to venture into the dark places of our lives, taking responsibility for how we will now live.

A very effective church-planter I knew started two thriving congregations. His apparent success covered the truth that his family was in turmoil, and that he suffered from a constant low-level depression. Finally he discovered that no amount of success could lighten the darkness. So, in time, he decided to open his long, invisible bag, where he uncovered several incidents of sexual abuse in his past. He realized that, from those terrible experiences on, he had determined never to be vulnerable again. His self-protective response was to become impenetrable — a relentless, tireless, hard-working man. He came to question what living like this did to his soul, to his marriage, and to his family. Though acknowledging that God worked both through him and despite him, he now questions the whole model of leadership he advocated and taught to many church leaders. He's traced his dark shadow backward, done the messy work, and is now living forward, with greater joy and depth than before.

But his story is not yours. Everyone's story is unique, and only you can discover what it means to trace the dark shadow into your past. Not everyone needs therapy. But I do think we all need to slow down and take a hard look at our lives at times. We don't want to be the people that the seventeenth-century Presbyterian pastor John Flavel describes: "There are some men and women who have lived forty or fifty years in the world and have had scarcely one hour's discourse with their hearts all the while."[4] Self-care isn't selfish. It's a vital part of becoming spiritually whole.

The great St. John of the Cross believed that each and every person — not only monks or the very spiritual — would necessarily experience a dark night of the soul, though some would choose to ignore it, thus missing its gift. But he also believed that because people are complex, each person would experience this dark night differently. A modern-day Carmelite monk writes, "To spiritual guides who might want to put people in boxes, [St. John] says that 'God carries each person along a different road, so that you will scarcely find two people following the same route in even half their journey to God.'"[5] St. John challenges us to walk with wisdom and patience into people's unique stories, finding what God will reveal in each. By moving toward the darkness rather than trying to manage or fix it, we move into a life freed from the enslavements of pride and possessions, of false securities of all kinds — a freedom that propels us into God's unique mission for each of us.

Understanding the Purpose of the Night

The dark night is not an invitation to endless suffering, but an invitation to transformation. But our fear of the dark can keep us from embracing its gift. F. LeRon Shults and Steven Sandage, a theologian and a psychologist writing on the dark night, describe it like this:

> Spiritual transformation often aborts early in the process because it is difficult to face the depths of darkness that threaten non-being; it is tempting to revert back into the comfortable sleepiness of life before the experience of awakening. It is precisely through the endurance of the darkness as one seeks for the promise of new being, however, that a person is opened up to the experience of the "illuminative" way. Here one experiences a new sense of joy and peace in the presence of God.[6]

In other words, the dark night tears at the very fabric of our carefully constructed realities, so much so that we're apt to choose a "comfortable sleepiness" rather than this paradoxical way of descent which leads to transformation. The dark night captures our deepest fear — a profound sense of feeling abandoned, alone, and anchorless in a tumultuous world. Who in their right mind would venture into this dark hole?

Some time ago I was at a party to celebrate a couple's fiftieth wedding anniversary. Their son sat down next to me. He seemed distraught considering that we were at a celebration for his parents. He said to me, "You know, Chuck, they've slept in separate beds for twenty years. We're celebrating a delusion." He went on to say that his mother's greatest fear was being alone. Yet, rather than walking down the dark road into her fear, she chose appeasement. And instead of dealing with his deep loneliness, her husband found refuge in adulterous relationships. Tragically, this is what happens when we ignore the dark night. Choosing to manage our pain, we set ourselves up for even deeper pain. St. John muses, "The more resolutions they make, the greater is their fall and the greater their annoyance, since they have not the patience to wait for that which God will give them."[7]

Daniel Schrock writes, "Our experience of emptiness, incredible though it may sound, indicates the powerful work of God hidden deep within us. Our despair testifies to hope, and our dying prepares us for spiritual growth."[8] The dark night ultimately opens us up to God's surgical knife, which cuts out whatever cancer diseases our souls. In the darkness we begin to see the truth about our false gods and fragile securities. The dark night offers the opportunity for greater freedom — freedom from the pretense of our futile attempts at managing our worlds, freedom from the chains of fear and control that enslave our hearts.

Thomas Merton, the great twentieth-century monk and spiritual writer, describes the tragedy of living an illusory life, which stifles our capacity to live and love:

> Every one of us is shadowed by an illusory person: a false self. This is the man I want myself to be but who cannot exist because God does not know anything about him. And to be unknown of God is altogether too much privacy. My false and private self is the one who wants to exist outside the reach of God's will and God's love . . . outside of reality and outside of life. And such a self cannot help but be an illusion. For most people in the world, there is no greater subjective reality than this false self of theirs, which cannot exist. A life devoted to the cult of this shadow is what is called a life of sin.[9]

Old Testament scholar Walter Brueggemann notes that without the dark night, even our worship is prone to a kind of "psychological inauthenticity." When the community of God gathers in disguise, with their masks and their public personas, worship is bound to be trivial, dishonest, and inauthentic.

Thus, when we live this illusory life, we live as false selves before one another, eroding our capacity to love God and love our neighbor. Our love is always contrived, contingent, and self-serving. Our churches and organizations become places where love cannot grow, thrive, and motivate mission. Our leadership becomes merely motivational, moralistic, and manipulative, inspiring for a moment but lacking the character to convey a deeper vision.

Embracing Our Own Dark Nights

At first, the darkness seems mysterious and unnerving. Who in his right mind would want to take this so-called adventure into scarier regions of his soul? While darkness may be relevant to monks and mystics, our intuition tells us to stay away from the dark.

A number of years ago, I led a church marriage retreat and called it "On the Death of Your Marriage" — a provocative title, to be sure! Fortunately, some people came anyway. While most couples came hoping to get the very best principles for a successful marriage, I came to tell them that the secret of their success was in examining the hairline cracks, the fears, and the battles of their lives together. I told them that until they got really honest about the mess they were in, change couldn't happen. I told them that their marriages would really begin to thrive as less noble versions of the "happy life" were forfeited. I told them that marriages, at some level, need to die to really live. Predictably, half the people in the room left feeling more hopeful than they ever had — for their marriages and for themselves. The other half left puzzled.

I expected that. After all, the dark night is counter-intuitive. It's paradoxical, and seems downright crazy. Who wants to die? I don't. In fact, I'll do everything I can to survive. My instincts tell me to kick, to scream, and to keep my head above water any way I can. And in the same way, the depression that creeps up on me at times sets off an alarm inside me that says, "Fix this. Take a pill. Tell yourself it isn't so bad. Just don't give in!" I may preach this stuff, but it's really hard to live.

But something still deeper within me (and I suspect within you, too) tells me that St. John was on to something. Looking around at the cheap fixes foisted on us by our culture and even by our churches, the old monk's wisdom breaks through with a strange, new kind of relevancy. It's just so crazy that it might work.

Leadership and management guru Robert Quinn agrees. Courageously, Quinn has abandoned much of the leadership thinking driven by success and achievement in favor of something more radical, something he calls "deep change." Quinn believes that leaders are trapped in predictable, life-sucking patterns that they are too prone to control and too fearful to change. He advocates "traveling naked into the land of uncertainty," calling for "individual transformation, a change of identity." He writes, "In embarking on the journey, we must leave the world of certainty. We must courageously journey to a strange place where there are a lot of risks and much is at stake, a place where there are new problems that require us to think in new ways."[10] Quinn tells leaders to face the dark.

But sometimes we don't actually choose this path; we get dragged down it through loss, pain, or failure. One pastor I knew moved to a medium-sized city, bringing within him what he thought was the recipe for success in his new congregation. In three years, he removed the pews, installed a projector and big screens, abandoned the old liturgy, and entirely overhauled the branding and culture of the church. In doing so, he effectively killed the church. Instead of drawing people, the changes prompted many to leave. In addition, the pastor was viewed as a charlatan among the tight-knit members of the community. And word got out. Within five years, he was selling cars. Grieved and empty, he faced his own dark night. He said to me, "Chuck, I grew up in that next year. I was an adolescent messing around with spiritual things. I had no business being a pastor. I think I might now be ready."

Jerry Sittser writes, "Deep sorrow often has the effect of stripping life of pretense, vanity, and waste. . . . It forces us to ask basic questions about what is most important in life. . . . That is why many people who suffer sudden and severe loss often become different people."[11] Through the dark night, we grow up. As Franciscan priest Richard Rohr puts it, we "fall upwards." About those who resist the dark night, he writes, "By denying their pain, avoiding the necessary falling, many have kept themselves from their own spiritual depths and therefore have been kept from their own spiritual heights."[12]

The dark night's invitation to look within assumes that there are large parts of us that have not been exposed to the strange illumination of the darkness. In order to lead others, we have to venture into the land of uncertainty, at the risk of dying. But in dying, as St. Paul says, we might find ourselves really living, perhaps for the first time (Gal. 2:20).

Embracing the World's Darkness

What is true for our own souls is also true of the dark and seemingly hopeless world we live in. But the same glory available to us in the dark night is available to the world we live in, if only we have a vision for it.

According to Daniel Schrock, "The dark night is a key part of God's missional purpose in the world."[13] It's a recognition that, like us, the world isn't what it's supposed to be. It's a revelation of the

ways in which our own radical selfishness, sabotage, and manipulation become externalized in the institutions and structures in
which we work and operate. Sadly, however, the world in which we
live plays the same game of self-deception that we play.

The dark night is an invitation not only to individuals, but
also to churches, to businesses, to institutions, and to nations to
take seriously the sin and brokenness in the world. It requires us
to acknowledge moments in our businesses, our churches, and in
our nation's story when the status quo is threatened and uncertainty lingers. I've often told leaders and pastors that times of
slow growth, stagnancy, or financial hardship can be dark nights,
opportune moments to ask God, "What are you stripping us of
right now?" Ignoring the dark night means that we are ignoring
God's persistent work of exposing and revealing the truth about
us and about the world in which we live.

Miroslav Volf writes,

> There can be no redemption unless the truth about the world is told and
> justice is done. To treat sin as if it were not there, when in fact it is there,
> amounts to living as if the world was redeemed when in fact it is not.
> The claim to redemption has degenerated into an empty ideology, and a
> dangerous one at that.[14]

Ignoring sin and brokenness in the world devalues God's redemptive purposes, and leaves us with a dangerous and empty
ideology, if not a dangerous and empty God. The God who loves
the world invites us to embrace its brokenness, acknowledge the
pretense, the deception, the injustice, the spin-doctoring, and the
image management that hounds our businesses, our churches, our
social systems, our political systems, and our financial systems.
Entering the dark night of the world then becomes an expression
of God's own incarnate love in Jesus Christ.

Embracing Darkness with Compassion

Finally, the dark night invites us to compassion. It recognizes that all of us wrestle with the false self, the parts of us that live out of deceit and pretense, the false narratives that propel our institutions and businesses. Typically, preachers and pundits enter our disappointments and failures not with compassion but with a message of judgment and wrath, lifting the gavel with a sentence of godlessness and incompetence. And we usually take it. We're a culture that's addicted to guilt.

I love the image of compassion painted by Susan Howatch in her great novel *Glittering Images.* Charles Ashworth is a man in need of compassion, an Anglican priest and canon who is sent by the Archbishop of Canterbury to do some investigative work on a controversial bishop. His journey into the seductively powerful world of church politics, however, exposes a deeper seduction within — an inner conflict which prevents him from seeing his world clearly, compelling him to live out of a false self — a "glittering image" committed to protecting him not only from the pain of his external world, but from the pain of his internal world. In a moment of crisis, Ashworth meets the compassionate Jon Darrow, a spiritual director who dares to ask about the self behind the glittering image. Darrow sees Ashworth for who he really is — a man burdened by the world's demands and his own internal demand to be successful.

Darrow, in our modern context, might emerge as a character who would judge Ashworth as a pastoral failure, sadly deficient for the high call of ministry. But Darrow is a man of compassion. Speaking to Ashworth's hidden, burdened self within, Darrow says, "He must be exhausted. Has he never been tempted to set down the burden by telling someone about it?"

"I can't," says Ashworth.

"Who's 'I'?" Darrow replies.

"The glittering image."

"Ah, yes," says Darrow, "and of course that's the only Charles Ashworth that the world's allowed to see, but you're out of the world now, aren't you, and I'm different from everyone else because I know there are two of you. I'm becoming interested in this other self of yours, the self nobody meets. I'd like to help him come out from behind that glittering image and set down this appalling burden which has been tormenting him for so long."

"He can't come out."

"Why not?"

"You wouldn't like him or approve of him."

"Charles, when a traveler's staggering along with a back-breaking amount of luggage, he doesn't need someone to pat him on the head and tell him how wonderful he is. He needs someone who'll offer to share the load."[15]

This story is a picture of compassionate confrontation with the dark night of the soul. Aware of the truth and grace hidden in dark places, Darrow is able to embrace the darkness instead of ignoring or attacking it. He sees Ashworth's condition as an opportunity, not an obstacle. And, he meets him in it not as a judge, but as a compassionate and curious friend interested in knowing and embracing every part of Ashworth, not merely his more appealing sides.

Compassion does not ignore the truth. It enters into it, wrestles with it. It requires a solidity and strength of relationship with others which endures even in times of extraordinary difficulty. It invites us to a cruciform life — a life lived in the pattern of the suffering servant. The compassion of the incarnate Christ was not some kind of cosmic Band-Aid administered from a distant parent, but a stupendous act of solidarity and love. This is our invitation as well.

Compassion requires us to descend into a broken world in need of hope. It leads us not only into our own brokenness but into the world's brokenness. It leads us to acknowledge the painful realities in our community — poverty, sex trafficking, addiction, depression, disease, and denial. It leads us to courageously invite hard conversations among our staffs, our community groups, those with whom we work and lead. It breeds the kind of honesty that is not only healthy, but attractive to a watching world that tends to see Christians as looking down their noses at the world's struggles.

For pastors and leaders, ignoring the dark night is comparable to ignoring reality. If we ignore the darkness in ourselves, others, and our world, we do not know ourselves, and we cannot possibly relate to or care for others or our world. We become impotent, unable to lead with a substantive vision. We become phonies, leading by technique rather than by character. Perhaps this is why the greatest leader of all time — Jesus himself — so often exposed the hypocrisy and hollowness of the religious and political leaders of his day.

And yet, Jesus gathered a team of ragamuffins, men and women not fit to lead, at least by the standards of his time. To them all, he said, "Follow me," knowing full well that this kind of following would require a unique cross for each (John 21:19). And so we, too, follow Jesus, tracing his steps along the narrow way which leads through a dark night. But the promise is that with each dark night, we emerge awakened to our own depths, inspired to meet the needs of a broken world, and enabled to lead with greater vision.

living with wholeness:
rest and resiliency in the leader's life

The genius of the biblical revelation is that it refuses to
deny the dark side of things, but forgives failure and
integrates falling to achieve its only promised wholeness.

RICHARD ROHR

Far too easily we settle for holiness rather than wholeness,
conformity rather than authenticity, becoming spiritual
rather than deeply human, fulfillment rather than
transformation, and a journey toward perfection rather
than union with God.

DAVID BENNER

The antidote to exhaustion is not rest but wholeheartedness.

DAVID WHYTE

May God himself, the God of peace, sanctify you through
and through. May your whole spirit, soul, and body be
kept blameless at the coming of our Lord.

1 THESSALONIANS 5:23

U P TO THIS point, most of what I've offered here might be summarized as "reflections on the divided heart." I've come to believe that much of what ails us today comes from the soul's deep fragmentation. Psychologists remind us that the psyche splits to survive pain. Neuroscientists tell us that pathology occurs when different parts of our brain fail to work in concord. Sociologists speak of the deep divisions between differing tribes. Family-systems theorists identify polarization within dysfunctional families. Educators and ethicists identify failures of integrity, or wholeheartedness, as a primary issue. And theologians speak of the divided heart. From different disciplines comes the same message, which is not surprising, since all truth is God's truth, no matter where you find it.

It's also a truth I engage every day, it seems, as I'm asked to consult on a variety of human problems and conflicts. The only stance that makes sense of the situation is that core assumption of the heart's dividedness and need for wholeness. It's also the core assumption of the Bible.

As a Christian, I operate from the premise that we're made in the image of God, created in and for original goodness and called into royal ambassadorship in the world on behalf of the King. I'm convinced, with many theologians, that sin shatters this image into many pieces. For Christians, what we call salvation is nothing less than the putting back together of the broken human soul and, beyond that, the broken and fragmented world in which we live. The gospel is "good news" — God is putting the world to rights, repairing deep divisions, mending broken hearts.

When Jesus said, "Blessed are the pure in heart, for they will see God" (Matt. 5:8), he was letting us in on this great secret of the undivided life. The word for purity in the original language might be translated "undivided." Those who can see God lack the inner divisions which plague and divide our souls. This is what the great Danish philosopher Søren Kierkegaard meant when he wrote,

"Purity of heart is to will one thing."[1] When our desires are refracted in a thousand different directions, we suffer the disease of division, which manifests itself in all kinds of spiritual and emotional ills. But the heart that is whole is being healed of its divisions, manifesting in a single spiritual current, rightly directed toward God and toward others in a way that brings healing rather than pain.

The great nineteenth-century preacher Charles Spurgeon diagnosed the divided heart as the most serious problem in the human soul. He wrote,

> [The divided heart] is a disease of a vital region — of the heart; a disease in a part so vital that it affects the whole man. The utmost extremity of the frame suffers when once the heart becomes affected, and especially so affected as to be divided. There is no power, no passion, there is no motive, no principle, which does not become vitiated, when once the heart is diseased.[2]

The ancient story of the first human beings fashioning clothing to hide their naked bodies (Gen. 3:7) also tells of this great psychological truth. Split from our true selves, we've fashioned elaborate cover-ups, false selves which, while they seem to help us to survive life's difficulties, actually cause personal and social fragmentation. The story continues — with Cain and Abel, Lamech, and a flood of judgment — to reveal how this dividedness sends fissures throughout all of life, like shattered safety glass. And that dividedness continues today. According to Parker Palmer, "The powers and principalities would hold less sway over our lives if we refused to collaborate with them. But refusal is risky, so we deny our own truth, take up lives of 'self-impersonation,' and betray our identities."[3] And when we do struggle to become whole, an array of cosmic forces rises up against us.

But a greater cosmic power has come to our rescue — Christ,

who is "the way, the truth, and the life" (John 14:6). In Christ, God has determined "to reconcile to himself all things, whether things on earth or things in heaven, by making peace through his blood, shed on the cross" (Col. 1:20), to sanctify us "through and through" so that we might become whole (1 Thess. 5:23). It's vital for us, personally, and for our leadership that we grasp this vision of human flourishing and wholeness for our lives and for the world around us.

Divided and Exhausted

At thirty-three, Deb shouldn't be this tired. She's an Ivy League graduate, a high achiever, and a devoted new Christian. But she's counting the days until retirement.

And she's not alone. I can spot exhaustion all over the place — walking down our city streets, in a Sunday-morning worship service, at Peet's Coffee, at my chiropractor's office. Everyone is busy. And tired. And counting the days until Friday, until the next vacation, until . . .

One glaring symptom of the divided heart is exhaustion. Why? It takes a lot of energy to drag that long, invisible bag behind us.

The Genesis story tells us that before the Fall, humankind experienced *shalom* — harmony, concord, flourishing in all manner of things. Now, we experience chaos, disorder, fragmentation. The woman with borderline personality disorder who harasses you with e-mails experiences this at a severe level. But you and I also experience it. Our exhaustion shows it. Sometimes we're so tired we don't know ourselves. We forget why we chose this job in the first place. We lose touch with our youthful idealism and innocence. We lose an original sense of passion we had for our work, our relationships, our religious life. We forget that childlike ability to approach God with anything. Eyes on the ground, just putting one foot in front of the other, we plod along, heedless of the glorious *shalom* for which we were created.

Rest: Not All It's Cracked Up to Be

Let's not kid ourselves — in both the corporate world and the church, we are measured by what we produce. I know few pastors today who aren't evaluated on the basis of the numerical growth and the financial stability of their congregations. I know few leaders not admired for their extraordinary success at growing their business or institution. I've seen my sister, one of the hardest workers I know, rise through the ranks of a major corporation, in large part because she's so devoted, loyal, and hard-working. Of course, hard productive work is good. God made us to work, and to accomplish good things. But when our identities become intertwined with our output, something is amiss.

When this happens, we become exhausted from our efforts. We live for our weekends and for our vacations. Convinced that we need rest, we plan a week's trip to the coast, or the mountains, or some dream destination. "All I need is a vacation," we say. "I'll come back refreshed." But we don't. In fact, our vacations and our weekends hold a hundred other anxieties. We've got to book the hotels, rent the cars, and manage the desire to overuse the credit card. We've got kids screaming, or e-mails piling up, or relationships straining. It's no wonder we sometimes think, *Thank God, I'm back at work! I need a vacation from my vacation!*

Rest is the most overused antidote to exhaustion today, and it hardly ever works. I know what the Bible says about rest, but I'm convinced we don't understand what rest really means.

An exhausted director of a nonprofit organization, David Whyte was pushing himself hard. Anyone working for such an organization knows the relentless pace, the constant demands, the endless fund-raising, and the never-ending needs. You can lose yourself in the frenzy of busyness, as Whyte once did. On an ordinary day at work, he walked into the break room and, without taking a moment to breathe, asked, "Has anyone seen David?"

David? His employees chuckled, almost embarrassed for him as he looked on, helpless. And then he realized what he'd done. Of course, he was speaking of himself, but he didn't even know it. In his exhaustion, he'd lost sight of himself and his calling.

That night, he sat with his friend, the Benedictine monk Father David Steindl-Rast. It was one of their regular poetry-reading evenings over glasses of wine. As Steindl-Rast was reading, Whyte interrupted him.

"Tell me about exhaustion," Whyte said.

Steindl-Rast responded, "You know that the antidote to exhaustion is not necessarily rest?"

"The antidote to exhaustion is not necessarily rest?" Whyte repeated woodenly. "What is it, then?" he asked.

His friend answered, "The antidote to exhaustion is wholeheartedness."[4]

Rest Revisited

We tend to define "rest" through our modern ideas. For many of us, rest, simply put, is not working. But the problem is this: our rest isn't that restful. We've missed the point of rest.

A favorite Jewish scholar of mine, Jacob Neusner, writes that God's command to rest is, in essence, an invitation to return to Eden in all its beauty, wholeness, and *shalom*.[5] For all the Christian chatter about "keeping Sabbath," I suspect most of us don't know what it means at all. We may define rest as stopping, sleeping, relaxing, enjoying — and all of these are very good! But we forget that we're literally incapable of rest if we're divided. Our inner divisions are what keep us from rest.

How often have you said, "It's just so hard to get away from work!" Perhaps it would be more honest to say, "I just can't get away from my busy, exhausted self!" I know this feeling well. For the first six years of pastoral ministry, I lived for my days off and vacations. The constant demands of those supervising my work and those I served gave me a kind of claustrophobic feeling. I wasn't sure where to go to get away. I began exploring spiritual disciplines, but without much direction I floundered. So I lived for the glorious two-week vacation to Iowa and the Ozarks with my wife's family each summer.

Still, each year I found myself irritated and aggravated as I began the vacation. I craved solitude. One year I took out my aggravation on my sister-in-law, whose fussy newborn frustrated my plans for total quiet and relaxation during our week of vacation at the lake house where we were staying. My sacred place was by the lake, with me in a chair with a good book. Anything that interrupted that cut into my fragile serenity. And anyone in the path of my irritation would pay.

As I write today, I'm at that same lake, many years later. And I'm much different. I feel whole and satisfied in my work. Vacation does not feel like an escape, from work or from people, as much as a privileged time to spend with family. I'm not counting the days until we go back. In fact, an occasional check of e-mail isn't a stressor, but a welcome connection to several colleagues I enjoy working alongside. So, what changed?

I changed.

You see, for some time I looked for the answer in a better supervisor, a better office space, a better laptop, a better paycheck, and better vacations. But the problem was my divided heart, and, as Spurgeon said, a heart divided is tantamount to *disease,* impacting every aspect of one's life. Tweaking a job description can help. A better supervisor may make our daily work more enjoyable. A better office space might give us the calm of being more organized. But none of these gets at the heart of human flourishing and wholeness. These minor shifts cannot re-orient our souls.

Wholeness can also be described as soulfulness, a life that's centered, passionately engaged, open, creative, connected, and propelled by a sense of mission. It is this kind of wholeness that leaders need to cultivate in themselves and in those under their leadership.

The best leaders do not focus merely on getting the most out of their people, but emphasize having a vision for their whole-hearted flourishing. They encourage wholeness where fragmentation exists. They instill passion where ambivalence exists. Peering into the divided souls of their people, they are able to tap hidden sources of energy. David Whyte writes,

> From the organizational side, if corporations ignore the darker underbelly of their employees' lives for a well-meaning approach, emphasizing only the positive, they will be forced to rely on expensive management pyramids to manipulate their workers at the price of commitment. Adaptability and native creativity on the part of the workforce come through the door only with their passions. Their passions come only with their souls. Their souls love the hidden springs boiling and welling at the center of existence more than they love the company.[6]

Motivational leadership is not enough, because too often it asks us to ignore darker parts of ourselves. On the other hand, leaders who have the courage to foster human flourishing invite into their organizations a wealth of passion and creativity — significant gifts that are often suppressed and ignored.

My brother-in-law Jeff runs a very successful dental practice with at least a dozen employees. Some time ago, he took a risk, hiring a young woman who showed some significant potential but who'd also experienced some difficulty in life. She did not come with an optimal background for a dental assistant. He hired her for her story, and what he saw of that story in her life — a healthy drivenness, a hunger to learn, a real sense of gratitude. Jeff wasn't afraid of a story which included dark valleys, but saw this as a crucible in which maturity and excellence could emerge. That's good leadership. And this young woman is not an employee who will merely crave the next vacation.

For me, greater wholeheartedness came through great pain and disappointment in my work, and a significant break-up in an important work relationship. Struggle and even failure drove me to look at my own heart more intentionally. I knew I needed to focus on my own brokenness and fragmentation rather than on the external factors that made me miserable. As Parker Palmer says, "Wholeness does not mean perfection: it means embracing brokenness as an integral part of life. Knowing this gives me hope that human wholeness — mine, yours, ours — need not be a utopian dream, if we can use devastation as a seedbed for new life."[7]

In my case, a friend and mentor saw beyond the turmoil and disorder, and passionately championed a new role for me that would more fully utilize my gifts. Unafraid of my many warts and quirks, he took a risk. I wouldn't be thriving today without his courageous leadership.

He was not afraid of the long, invisible bag that I dragged behind me, but saw within it untapped creativity as well as unforgiven darkness. In encouraging me along the way, he didn't settle for motivation, but sought integrity. Palmer reminds us of what happens when we don't allow ourselves to be revealed:

> Afraid that our inner light will be extinguished or our inner darkness exposed, we hide our true identities from each other. In the process, we become separated from our own souls. We end up living divided lives, so far removed from the truth we hold within that we cannot know the integrity that comes from being what you are.[8]

It's easy for leaders to ignore the dark side, and get the most out of the false selves of their people. Our false selves crave affirmation, and manipulative and motivational leaders can prey on the insecurities of the false self to get results. Healthy leaders refuse to settle for cheap tactics. They see health and wholeness as integral to the bigger mission. They foster a spirit of independence and creativity in people who live from a deeper, more secure core — the true self. This self does not obsess about the next vacation or manipulate the time card. It does not selfishly seek promotion. Rather, the true self rests in a larger identity as the beloved of God, approved of in a way that transcends promotion or pay. The true self is the whole self, whose rest and whose work is imbued with integrity, creativity, passion, and spiritual energy.

Wholeness and Healing

To become whole, we need to be healed, and this takes a lifetime. Wholeness cannot be delivered in a three-point sermon or a self-help lecture. Wholeness, instead, is invited. Invited and envisioned, it grows and ripens, and its fruits begin to spill over in ways that demonstrate the presence of the kingdom.

But as Richard Rohr writes, deep healing sometimes also requires major surgery. It's a process in which mind, heart, and body require re-orientation and re-integration:

> Mere mental belief systems split people apart, whereas actual faith puts all our parts (body, heart, head) on notice and on call, and offers us a new broadband station, with full surround sound, instead of a static-filled monotone. Honestly, it takes major surgery and much of one's life to get head, heart, and body to put down their defenses, their false programs for happiness, and their many forms of resistance to what is right in front of them. This is the meat and the muscle of the whole conversion process.[9]

This is not merely a self-improvement project. While it requires certain disciplines — Bible reading, church attendance, weekly meetings — they cannot produce real transformation. The biblical pattern is clear: one must go through a wilderness to discover the promised land.[10]

In God's economy of grace, the way to healing is not around the pain, but through it. And it's in the going-through that you and I become more like Christ, more whole and more human. In following Christ along the wilderness way, we become open to a radical, holistic transformation, one that promises that our "false programs for happiness" will be destroyed.

My friend Hal courageously gave up a very lucrative career to do what he loved. Trusting that the life of wholeheartedness was more important than the rat race he was living, he started a new venture, a small business geared to building relationships among wine lovers, and providing them with greater knowledge and a better, healthier experience of enjoying the gift of wine. That doesn't sound like major surgery, but what Hal couldn't foresee were the hardships that would come when the honeymoon ended. Battling a sinking economy and seismic internal shifts in the company, Hal has been journeying through a valley for some time now — a valley not without beams of light, but nevertheless one that has brought great self-reflection and hard inner work. Hal's glittering false self, once nurtured by success in the corporate world, is dying yet another death, as a man whose profound faith and remarkable maturity grow a true self in the rich soil of difficulty.

The Healing Power of Confession

For a priest, the ancient practice of confession was a sacred encounter, an opportunity to divulge one's deepest secrets in the context of a healing, forgiving relationship. Celtic priests challenged the medieval hierarchy of their day by making confession more universally available, questioning the notion that bishops alone could forgive sins, and empowering all priests to hear the confessions of the people.[11] This was a radical notion, one that humanized the sacrament and made forgiveness more widely available. It took Martin Luther to further radicalize the practice, empowering the "priesthood of all believers" to hear one another's confessions. In these earlier days, confession was crucially important to a believer's life, part of the core of Christian worship and, most important, central to human growth and change.

By privatizing confession, the church abdicated its role in publicly embracing the sinner with the forgiving arms of Christ. The therapeutic community stepped in to fill the gap.[12] Psychologists like Freud and Jung examined the subconscious, the darker parts of the human personality. And what they found did not necessarily contradict Christian assumptions. What they found was that the human "shadow" side needed an outlet, a voice, a way into the light. The darkness needed light.

Bill Wilson, who founded Alcoholics Anonymous, brought this ancient spirituality back to the masses in his Twelve-Step program.

Men and women suffering from addiction gathered in small groups in church basements. Sitting on folding chairs, they acknowledged their powerlessness before God and their addicted peers. Each addict proceeded through the early steps into the difficult waters of the fourth step: make a searching and fearless moral inventory of ourselves. Wilson, of course, was mining the depths of Augustine and Calvin, and their own fearless admonitions to self-reflection. Curiously, this healing was not only for the addict alone. The addict's healing would be a gift to her community as she, in turn, would become a sponsor to others.

James, the brother of Jesus, writes, "Therefore confess your sins to each other, and pray for each other, so that you may be healed" (James 5:16). Healing requires confession, it seems. And in opening our "dark side" to the light, we abandon the self-help techniques which keep us from wholeness and transformation. Parker Palmer writes,

> The divided life is a wounded life, and the soul keeps calling us to heal the wound. Ignore that call, and we find ourselves trying to numb our pain with an anesthetic of choice, be it substance abuse, overwork, consumerism, or mindless media noise. Such anesthetics are easy to come by in a society that wants to keep us divided and unaware of our pain.[13]

To create a healthy environment of wholeheartedness, leaders need to be unafraid of the darkness within. When we openly "confess" our own failures and fears, we can create an atmosphere in which honesty and acceptance help people become more whole by refusing to sidestep the wilderness within. By fostering an atmosphere of openness to the dark sides of ourselves, we bring the light of grace and truth into the darkness, dispelling some of its grip. Ignoring that inner darkness further divides the soul, wounding it even more deeply. Acknowledging it and inviting it in create a

space for healing and transformation which, in turn, can be the fuel
for corporate transformation.

Your Mission as a Leader
(Should You Choose to Accept It) . . .

The peril of leadership is this: You lead a mass of contradictions.
I've heard countless stories of leaders who have done their home-
work when hiring a new employee, including background checks,
personality tests, and reference calls. But after six months, the
employee seems entirely different, grumbling and complaining,
causing disruption and killing morale. Pastors tell stories of the
extraordinary parishioner who comes promising to give sacrificially
and serve wholly. But, in time, this person becomes a thorn in the
pastor's side. One leader who resigned recently told me, "I expected
some bumps. I didn't expect to be pummeled."

David Benner explains what leaders are up against:

> Despite the rhetoric, transformation is seldom truly desired by most
> Christians or welcomed by most churches. Most of us prefer to keep the
> change process under our control and limited to the small tinkerings as-
> sociated with our self-improvement projects. If we are genuinely open to
> the unfolding of self that is involved in transformation, we will generally
> encounter resistance in most of the places that we normally expect support.
> Families, community, and culture often conspire to keep us safely in a
> place of conformity. As noted by Richard Rohr, most religion — and this
> certainly includes Christianity — is more tribal than transformational.[14]

Leadership is difficult. We're tugged at from all sides by people
who want their perspective affirmed, or their agenda adopted, or
their beliefs validated. We're tempted to please people rather than

cast vision, tempted to become a yes-man rather than making the hard call. Most of all, we're tempted to settle, time and again, for smaller visions rather than the big, transformative vision of God's kingdom invading our lives.

As a leader, I've often made the mistake of thinking that my own success was predicated on meeting people's needs. I've crafted sermons based on what I thought people would like. I've made decisions to appease. I've caved in to criticism. But too often, while attracting a crowd, I've created chaos.

I've recently discovered that the "crowd," in the Gospels, was a negative thing, not a positive one. The crowd was generally whiny and disruptive to a prophetic Jesus. The way of success for Jesus was telling the truth, even if it hurt. He put words to the inner division of the religious elite, calling them "hypocrites" and "white-washed tombs," polished on the outside but rotting on the inside (Matt. 23:27). Seldom have I been so bold about confronting divisive people.

But I'm learning that people crave honesty from their leaders. They want us to tell the truth, even if it hurts a bit. Of course, that doesn't include shaming and put-downs. We need to tell the truth from our own place of wholeness, honest about our own blindness and faults. But from a place of humility, we can speak to others with vision and with courage, calling them to live into their deepest identity as "new creations" in Christ.

I think of leaders like Martin Luther King Jr. and his namesake, Martin Luther. I'm inspired by St. John of the Cross and Teresa of Ávila, Thomas Merton and Dorothy Day. Each proclaimed that the God who'd taken up residence in their hearts and cleaned house was also the God who reconciled polarized groups, challenged religious tribalism, and confronted inner divisions. I want to be this kind of leader.

I'm increasingly convinced that whether you lead a church or a car wash, whether you run an insurance company or an animal shelter, real leadership requires wholeness, and real leadership invites wholeness in others. Anything less is a cheap imitation, a motivational game or a self-improvement project that does nothing more than decorate the outside without reordering the inside.

Christian psychologist David Benner describes the challenge of this more radical transformation:

> Far too easily we settle for holiness rather than wholeness, conformity rather than authenticity, becoming spiritual rather than deeply human, fulfillment rather than transformation, and a journey toward perfection rather than union with God. Far too often we confuse our own spiritual self-improvement tinkerings with the much more radical agenda of the Spirit of God. The call of the Spirit — which is always gentle and therefore easily missed — is an invitation to abandon our self-improvement projects that are, in reality, little more than polishing our false self and become the unique hidden self in Christ that we have been from all eternity. The call of the Spirit is always a call to return home, to settle for no other habitation or identity than that of being in Christ and knowing the reality of Christ in us.[15]

CHAPTER 8

growing into leadership maturity: self-care and the art of shadow-boxing

> Most leaders focus on how to succeed in a task. A far better approach is to focus on who you are.
>
> WES GRANBERG-MICHAELSON

> God is love. When we take up permanent residence in a life of love, we live in God and God lives in us. This way, love has the run of the house, becomes at home and mature in us.
>
> 1 JOHN 4:17 (THE MESSAGE)

> Believe the incredible truth that the Beloved has chosen for his dwelling place the core of your own being because that is the single most beautiful place in all of creation.
>
> ST. TERESA OF ÁVILA

MANY ARE FAMILIAR with the oft-repeated story about G. K. Chesterton, the great British writer and journalist who was once asked by a British newspaper to share his thoughts about the big issues of the day. It was a complicated time in turn-of-the-century England, and Chesterton had the opportunity to add his thoughts to those of a stunning lineup of other writers and thinkers. As a brilliant wordsmith and bold personality, he had been given the perfect setup for a well-executed, brilliant editorial piece.

And yet, to the very pointed question "What's wrong with the world?," Chesterton replied, "I am."

Today, corporate leaders are chiming in, adding contemporary credibility and challenging those who see self-knowledge as mere psychological mumbo-jumbo, or Christian self-flagellation. Leadership expert Robert Quinn, for example, notes that the price of avoiding deep, personal change is "the choice of slow death, a meaningless and frustrating experience enmeshed in fear, anger, and helplessness, while moving surely toward what is most feared."[1] And even a guru of leadership technique like Marshall Goldsmith recognizes the ultimate cost of a lack of self-knowledge: "After living with their dysfunctional behavior for so many years (a sunk cost if ever there was one), people become invested in defending their dysfunctions rather than changing them."[2]

A personal hero and mentor of mine, Wesley Granberg-Michaelson, has for decades been a leader in the world of politics, nonprofits, and the church. He has been the Director of Church and Society for the World Council of Churches, and the General Secretary of the Reformed Church in America. He writes,

> Most leaders focus on how to succeed in a task. A far better approach is to focus on who you are. It is said that the unexamined life is not worth living. Certainly, the unexamined life is unequipped for leading, and the cost of leaders who act blindly or in denial of their own weakness is devastating. People suffer needlessly. Trust is betrayed. Entire organizations can be crippled.[3]

If he is right, then when we focus on who we are with integrity, much of the rest takes care of itself. I wouldn't want to diminish the importance of needed skills and acumen. But some of the most skilled pastors I've known have also been some of the most danger-ous — self-righteous, brash, and angry. If asked, I'd recommend a pastor with less skill but great character and integrity rather than the skilled pastor lacking these vital things.

We have work to do as leaders, work Richard Rohr calls "shadow-boxing."[4] With the necessary humility that leads to wisdom, we can and will mature. And this maturity in character will allow us to admit further deficiencies — needed places of growth in skill and ability. It is the risky and courageous work of opening that long, invisible bag we drag behind us, and doing business with it. It requires facing those false selves we've developed that cause us to become tough, defensive, charismatic, cunning, or even sinister. In time, God invites us to face ourselves, to "shadow-box" in a ring in which we fight an inner war, as St. Paul called it (Rom. 7), battling our flesh (false self) and being strengthened in spirit (true self). Rohr believes that because we are wounded in the context of relationship, we can be healed only in the context of relationship, in the boxing ring with God.

In this chapter we'll explore several disciplines for shadow-boxing, the leader's work of self-care, growth, and maturity. But don't hear the word "disciplines" as a reference to mere behaviors. Too often, self-care is reduced to a series of self-help steps which trivialize the depth and complexity of human growth and maturity. Both the pain we encounter and the healing we find occur in the context of relationship. The real fix, if there is one, is being found by God, often with the help of others whom you trust. Behavior modification might change a particular pattern in your life, but relationship literally changes you — your very being, including the hardwiring of your brain.

This insight is not merely biblical or theological, but affirmed by both brain scientists and psychologists. Curt Thompson, a Christian and a neuropsychologist, observes, "It is only when we are known that we are positioned to become conduits of love. And it is love that transforms our minds, makes forgiveness possible, and weaves a community of disparate people into the tapestry of God's family."[5] We complain in protest, "There must be another way! I'd rather be fixed than found — being known seems too difficult!" And yet, with the evidence of brain science firmly in mind, Thompson continues,

> There is no other way. To be known is to be pursued, examined, and shaken. To be known is to be loved and to have hopes and even demands placed on you. It is to risk, not only the furniture in your home being rearranged, but your floor plans being rewritten, your walls being demolished and reconstructed. To be known means that you allow your shame and guilt to be exposed — in order for them to be healed.[6]

The prescription here is not a series of behavior modifications for that illusive "happier and healthier you." That is the American myth. What I suggest, instead, are disciplines — which recalls the word "disciple" — a follower of Christ. Disciplines place us in relationship — with Christ and within a community of wounded healers. The discipline of a disciple is to follow — that is, to walk in the shadow of Christ, to learn his ways, to struggle together when difficulties arise, to laugh and to cry. This is how friendship with God unfolds, as a relationship between two persons deeply committed to each other in covenant love. This relationship cannot be reduced to a mere practice or ritual, but it certainly involves practice and ritual — the give and take required in any relationship. I'm convinced that as we know and are known by God, love and are loved by God — the sum of the Commandments, according to Jesus — we will experience a deeper, more sustained flourishing in our life and leadership.

Discipline 1: The Mirror of Real Friendship

A leader's maturity may be directly correlated to the health of her relationships.

Paradoxically, leaders often isolate themselves out of fear. Some of the most powerful leaders today are relationally impotent, fed from the fumes of an insecure false self rather than the fuel of honest relationship. Even some of the more seemingly "relational" and charismatic leaders know how to *communicate* to people, but don't know how to *relate* to people.

Self-care for the leader might begin with this basic question to two or three colleagues or friends: How do you experience me? I asked that question many years ago in a group of good friends. The answers I received were frightening. The words included "arrogant," "intimidating," "insecure," "shallow," and "angry." I had no response. Stunned, I dropped my head, and I began to tear up. In another time, I may have been defensive. But this time I was a bit more ready, tired of the persona that I'd lived from.

How would people respond to you? One leader recently told me that his colleagues responded only affirmingly. I told him that I'd rarely seen feedback without some critique. And so I asked him to go back and remind his colleagues that they could speak the truth, with no repercussions. When he returned, his head hung low, too. They had used words like "untrustworthy," "unreliable," and "cranky." I asked him if they were wrong. Humbly, he responded with a very simple answer: "No." However, that day proved to be the launching pad for significant personal change for him, and profound maturity as a leader.

Parker Palmer emphasizes the importance of community in this endeavor to grow:

> A strong community helps people develop a sense of true self, for only in community can the self exercise and fulfill its nature: giving and taking, listening and speaking, being and doing. . . . Lacking opportunities to be ourselves in a web of relationships, our sense of self disappears, leading to behaviors that further fragment our relationships and spread the epidemic of inner emptiness.[7]

Palmer suggests that leaders create "circles of trust," small and safe groups where they can know and be known.

Do you have relationships that cultivate honesty and transparency? Are there at least a few people in your life who can challenge you? I lament when people answer, "No, I've never really been challenged," or "I've never really been known." Often it takes just one real friendship, one real taste of being known, in order to awaken a deeper hunger to be known fully by God.

It was King David whose relational emptiness and loneliness led him to solicit, even demand, another man's wife, an act not just of adultery but of manipulation and abuse. As if this wasn't enough, he commanded that her husband be murdered so that he could take the woman as *his* wife. (I'm not sure that many pastors or leaders today could survive a scandal of this magnitude.) It took what I'd consider to be a real friend — Nathan — to awaken David to the depth of his alienation from God and from his truest self (2 Samuel 12). Once awakened, David acknowledged his sin. Now, I don't think that his acknowledgment was merely behavioral ("I did something bad"); it was relational ("I've violated trust"). Sin, in fact, is alienation from God and, consequently, alienation from our own image-bearing core. David recognized that he'd strayed far from his deepest identity and core relationship.

This is what makes his prayer in Psalm 139 so telling:

You have searched me, Lord,
  and you know me.
You know when I sit and when I rise;
  you perceive my thoughts from afar.
You discern my going out and my lying down;
  you are familiar with all my ways.
Before a word is on my tongue
  you, Lord, know it completely.
You hem me in behind and before,
  and you lay your hand upon me.
Such knowledge is too wonderful for me,
  too lofty for me to attain.
Where can I go from your Spirit?
  Where can I flee from your presence?
If I go up to the heavens, you are there;
  if I make my bed in the depths, you are there.
If I rise on the wings of the dawn,
  if I settle on the far side of the sea,
even there your hand will guide me,
  your right hand will hold me fast.
If I say, "Surely the darkness will hide me
  and the light become night around me,"
even the darkness will not be dark to you;
  the night will shine like the day,
  for darkness is as light to you.

The mirror of real friendship, including friendship with God, is one which is unafraid of the dark, as David says in the last verse. By inviting others into our darkness, we are known, and in being known, we are healed.

Discipline 2: The Gift of Solitude

Leadership expert Robert Quinn writes,

> When we see the need for deep change, we usually see it as something that needs to take place in someone else. In our roles of authority, such as parent, teacher, or boss, we are particularly quick to direct others to change. Such directives often fail, and we respond to the resistance by increasing our efforts. The power struggle that follows seldom results in change or brings about excellence. One of the most important insights about the need to bring about deep change in others has to do with where deep change actually starts.[8]

There is one place where we cannot project all of our experiences on to another. It is the place of solitude. Solitude, instead of being a lonely place, is a relationally rich place where we discover who we really are.

Many of us struggle being alone. Addicted to the noise and busyness of life, we'd much prefer sitting with another and chatting about sports, fashion, market fluctuations, or the annoying idiosyncracies of our colleagues. Alone, we're tempted to turn on the television, open the laptop, or check our texts — anything to avert our gaze from ourselves.

I've heard many criticize American culture, and even American Christians, as self-consumed. I beg to differ. I see people who are afraid of themselves. At the very least, the "self" they are feeding is a false self, a starving child addicted to attention, affirmation, or adoration. More accurately, I believe people are more often self-contemptuous. They are not just afraid of themselves, but ashamed of themselves. And true solitude puts them — puts us — in a certain encounter with the self they/we are scared to meet.

Henri Nouwen describes the difficulty of solitude:

As soon as we are alone, inner chaos opens up in us. This chaos can be so disturbing and so confusing that we can hardly wait to get busy again. Entering a private room and shutting the door, therefore, does not mean that we immediately shut out all our inner doubts, anxieties, fears, bad memories, unresolved conflicts, angry feelings, and impulsive desires. On the contrary, when we have removed our outer distractions, we often find that our inner distractions manifest themselves to us in full force. We often use the outer distractions to shield ourselves from the interior noises. This makes the discipline of solitude all the more important.[9]

You don't have to be a mystic to experience the benefits of solitude. You need only make yourself available, learning to cultivate a quiet, interior space. Yes, this takes practice. On a silent retreat, I'll often sit in a chapel or by a lake for a long while before the interior noise begins to settle. The first thing I'll notice is my breath. I'm often surprised and comforted by mere breathing, as I'm often breathlessly busy. Sitting quietly and attentively, I'll imagine a space opening up within me, receptive to God's breath. As my soul gradually opens, I begin to feel a weight lift. Perhaps this is where Jesus says to each of us, "My yoke is easy, and my burden is light."

In this place, you discover that core, deepest self that I've been talking about. You may find that he or she is a stranger. After periods of solitude, I've often ended up thinking, *Welcome back, Chuck.* Tugged in so many directions and triggered to live out of my many well-developed false selves, I'm eager to get to know what theologians call my God-self, where the Spirit dwells.

One of my favorite Christian mystics, St. Teresa of Ávila, speaks beautifully of this place. In her classic work, *The Interior Castle,* she describes our innermost soul as

a secret place. A radiant sanctuary. As real as your own kitchen. More real than that. Constructed of the purest elements. Overflowing with ten thousand beautiful things. Worlds within worlds. Forests, rivers. Velvet coverlets thrown over featherbeds, fountains bubbling beneath a canopy of stars. Bountiful forests, universal libraries. A wine cellar offering an intoxication so sweet you will never be sober again. A clarity so complete you will never again forget. This magnificent refuge is inside you. Enter. Shatter the darkness that shrouds the doorway. . . . Believe the incredible truth that the Beloved has chosen for his dwelling place the core of your own being because that is the single most beautiful place in all of creation.[10]

If we were to believe this to be true, it would destroy our false selves. If we, as Christians, were to believe that God has taken up residence within us by the Spirit and calls us a "temple," we might dare to believe that who we are, at our deepest core, is worth sharing with the world.

We are the influencers. Our impact is felt by many who choose to place trust in us as pastor, manager, boss, team leader, bishop, or CEO. As we more deeply and regularly meet God in prayerful solitude, we find that the same love that invaded our hearts is available to others.

Solitude begins with a simple recognition — that we are not the selves we project or even inflict on others, but souls breathed into life by God. Inviting that breath to once again animate us, we find ourselves at home in the God who loves *us,* not some caricature of us.

Discipline 3: The Rhythm of Worship

For five years I was a teaching pastor at a San Francisco church packed with busy, upwardly mobile twenty- to thirty-somethings. In a city like San Francisco, the weekends hold great promise for snow and skiing in Tahoe, outdoor festivals, exciting nightlife, and more. I was thrilled that so many made Sunday worship a priority in the most secular city in the United States; still, there were others who placed regular worship further down in priority, given their exhausting work responsibilities and all the diverting possibilities the city offers.

But I also noticed another phenomenon. Though the number of gray-haired folks were fewer overall, they seemed to make attendance a priority. And so I started asking them why. And what I heard was encouraging. These were not your traditional, guilt-ridden, "I've got to be at church" kinds of Christians. Rather, they were mature enough to know their deep need to rest and to relax into God's welcoming arms. They were hungry for the weekly rhythms of offering confession, listening to the Word, and bringing their deep hunger and thirst to the Eucharistic table. Many of them once knew a life where they were pulled in different directions, constantly competing, continually looking for the next adventure, compelled to always be on the move. Now they looked at the younger men and women around them and smiled, quite aware that they, too, once played that game. But now, they could not miss worship.

Why? One man told me, "Worship invites me into the Grand Story, making every other story in which I find my identity a cheap imitation." Another man, just beyond the frontier of forty, told me, "I'm so much more aware of my need to simply sit in God's presence for at least an hour each week. Sometimes, I don't even hear the sermon. But I'm there, at least."

In worship, we are invited into an alternative reality.[11] Because our lives are narrated by the cultural and personal stories we live in, we can get stuck, bound by the rat race of a corporate culture or the thrill of the next experience. Worship invites us into an alternative Story where our lives find a center in relationship to God, where we are "sons," "daughters," and "the beloved," not merely CEOs, managers, and leaders.

Now, a word to pastors. I do recognize that you're faced with an entirely different level of complexity, at this point, as you lead worship. Your "false self" can be on full display in worship. You can feel desperately alone on Sundays. And because of this, many good books and articles advise you to take your own Sabbaths, to find rest in different ways, to worship privately. While that's true, this practice should not be an escape, but should create an opportunity for you to engage in public worship with a healthier spirit. As you grow and mature, you find that you too can be true participants in worship. You find that you need to be there, just as others do. You find that you need to confess, to hear the gospel, to commune with Christ and his Body.

If your false self is on display each Sunday, you need help. Don't think you'll somehow magically discover health without some genuine inner work. Have the courage that many other pastors have had and take your situation seriously. St. Augustine took his sexual addiction seriously. Samuel Rutherford took his grief seriously. Charles Spurgeon took his depression seriously. And each is considered a hero in church history. Be the kind of hero that finds strength in weakness, and trust that God will meet you.

Discipline 4: The Freedom to Break the Rules

In our clock-in, clock-out culture, we're not used to much freedom or flexibility in our workplaces. As leaders, many of us get our game faces on as we're entering the office, and we often find it hard to relax afterwards. Many of us have risen to a place of leadership because of our self-discipline and a relentless work ethic. For us, productivity requires constant acceleration, and any let-up can hurt the bottom line, whether it's a financial bottom line or the number of people who show up to church each Sunday.

Rather than radically disrupting the leaders whom I work with by suggesting a sabbatical or a major lifestyle change, I begin with a simple prescription: break the rules each day. Here's what I mean. I've seen the benefits when leaders choose to do something out of the ordinary, whether restful or adventurous, to "disrupt" the false self and cultivate a new way of being.

A rule-breaker that I've occasionally practiced is the power nap. As a native New Yorker, I remember our former mayor — Ed Koch — taking a nap each day at work. It seemed a bit silly until I learned that Albert Einstein, Winston Churchill, Harry Truman, and other great thinkers and leaders often practiced this same habit. So I've encouraged others to do the same. I'll never forget a colleague's look when I suggested he go into one of our therapy rooms, shut off the light, and nap for a bit. As the father of a newborn, he'd been coming into the office with bloodshot eyes, and I'd sometimes see him staring off into space. When he'd catch me looking at him, he'd immediately rouse himself and resume working. After all, his false self was whispering, "It's not good to let your boss see you like this." So I simply disrupted his false self. I told him to take a nap during work hours. After that, he felt much freer to be himself in the office, and I suspect he began to see me as someone who cared rather than someone who merely used him.

In the Bay Area, many of the local tech companies provide a healthy lunch each day, snacks, and even free transportation to and from work. A friend of mine who leads a tech startup told me, "If I create a healthy and happy work environment, people are apt to be creative and excited to be at work." Another local leader buys his staff coffee each mid-morning, and often stops by people's desks randomly, just to check in. I asked one of his employees what happened in the frequent desk-side meet-and-greets, and she said, "He asks about my life. He wants to know what I need to thrive.

He checks to see if there's anything that the company can do better to thrive in its mission."

Today, many call this wisdom in practice the "Triple Bottom Line" — the bottom lines of profit, planet, and people. In a disconcerting twist once again, the corporate world seems to practice this Triple Bottom Line better than the church. Perhaps this perception has a lot to do with the progressive area that I live in; still, it's heartening to see executives sacrificing pure profit for environmental stewardship and organizational health and satisfaction.

The discipline of "breaking the rules" isn't mere behavior modification, though it may seem that way. I see this daily disruption as a gateway to an intrusion — an intrusion of grace and of awareness, which leads to relationship. The simple nap my co-worker took opened him up to the very real understanding that he wasn't a machine meant to clock in and clock out each day, but an image-bearer, designed for dignity by God, meant to thrive and flourish. This simple act awakened him to a deeper need for rest, and reminded him that he was known, at least by me.

Likewise, the intrusions of grace within the workplace which include lunch, snacks, or even a weekly debrief convey a sense of personal value — they say, in effect, "We know you, we respect you, and we value what you do." And as neuropsychologists have found, these simple reminders that we are known truly do rewire our brains, contributing to our health and wholeness as human beings.

Pastors, too, need to experience regular disruptions like these and others. We are more apt to take ourselves too seriously than people in almost any other vocation. But there's a reason for that. Most ordained pastors recognize after some time in ministry that they are always "on" — because the phone can ring at any hour with a crisis call, because there is always more to pray, because each Sunday brings the relentless return of worship and sermon preparation. Recently I counseled a pastor to "break the rules"

— to cancel his afternoon study time and go see a movie. He felt as if he was violating something sacred. He told me later that he felt embarrassed buying the ticket, and even more embarrassed getting a bucket of popcorn. He hadn't told anyone, not even his wife, of his plans.

But after watching the movie, this normally stoic, well-disciplined pastor began to cry. He'd seen a film which was especially stirring, particularly because he was a pastor in the South. It was the 2011 movie *The Help*, winner of many awards that year. On a day when he did what seemed unpardonable — seeing a movie in the middle of the afternoon — he was awakened to the seemingly unpardonable, a history of racial injustice and relational violence that pierced him to the core. He told me that he sobbed for five minutes at the end of the movie, unable to leave his seat. And he said that something within him was released afterward, as if his eyes were opened to see life in a new way. "I'd never seen the implications of the gospel in such depth and clarity before," he explained. "It was like the veil fell and I could finally see."

In a simple act of breaking the rules, my friend experienced God's disruptive and loving grace.

Discipline 5: The Practice of Daily Prayer

Our daily habits and rhythms say much about what is going on in our souls. I need only notice how I slip into the morning ritual of checking ESPN, Twitter, or the news online to see where my attention is. The necessary shadow-boxing begins as I confront my own tendency to turn my attention to entertainment and consciously turn back to my own humanity, awakened each morning with a need to find its center and rest in God.

Though my practices shift from season to season, I attempt to make it a regular discipline to pray using historic and well-worn liturgies to meet God. During certain seasons, I tend to practice the Daily Office.[12] The Office (or service) is a regular cycle of prayer which can be used at various times of the day. In the Office, the participant is invited to enter and end with silence, while reading portions of Scripture, many psalms, prayers of confession, and texts from wise souls from church history. I also gravitate toward the Daily Examen, inspired by St. Ignatius of Loyola. The version I use is a more contemporary form, but the point is the same.[13] The Examen invites the participant to read Scripture and reflect on his life — how he experiences God, how he's feeling, where he's struggling. The Examen brings the participant into an even more intentional shadow-boxing ring.

On other occasions, I seek out a prayer labyrinth.[14] To many evangelicals, the labyrinth looks like a maze, or perhaps some New Age technique for spiritual awareness. However, the Christian labyrinth is an ancient way of walking the way of the Cross and meeting God. As one walks to the center of the labyrinth, one is invited to process one's life internally, laying down certain inner idols and attachments which constrict the soul and sap life. In the center, one takes as much time as one needs to meet God in silence. I am often struck by how raw my soul finds itself in this simple inner ring, where I'm sometimes surrounded by others walking the path, or by the chattering of tourists visiting the picturesque cathedral. The journey out of the center of the labyrinth brings its own shadow-boxing challenge, as I am invited to examine how I will live more intentionally and contemplatively in my public life. Each January, I take Bay Area leaders on a silent spiritual retreat where we practice the labyrinth, among other disciplines, and I'm often told it is one of the most powerful times of self-reflection and prayer.

Our greatest enemy in this is our busyness, of course. Well-intentioned pastors often find that this practice is eclipsed in the face of appointments, sermon preparation, and meetings. I've often found that I must schedule these things on my calendar. If someone asks for time, I can simply say, "My calendar does not permit it."[15] Now I am challenging you to an intentional practice of the presence of God, which can take many different forms. Form is not the issue. Intention is.[16]

I've had to shadow-box with that distracted part of me, which craves time on the couch with my attentive companion, ESPN. The drama of sports can capture my attention with a force that overwhelms my better instincts. I simply have to know the latest news about the NFL, or the score of last night's San Francisco Giants game. Beyond that, I'm drawn in to the newest craze, a kind of sports gossip which might be the equivalent of a soap opera or tabloid story. Over time, I find my soul crammed with trivia in a way that crowds out God and stifles prayer.

Daily prayer recenters my soul, though not without a fight. The shadow-boxing ring is full of activity during these times. Because my soul is so addicted to its remedies for daily peace and happiness, I'm compelled to wrestle with God, making these daily prayer times far more than a simple routine or ritual. Of course, there are days when daily prayer may feel ordinary, and that's all right. The goal is not to experience something profound each time, but rather to engage God. I see it in much the same way that I see eating dinner around the table with my family every night. Not every evening will bring stirring conversation. But the practice of gathering cultivates an opportunity for connection and for relationship, even if nothing obviously significant happens.

As we become more familiar with sitting in the presence of God, we realize that what is most significant may actually be happening beneath the surface. That is the power of this practice, the real power of prayer.

Benediction

A benediction is a blessing. Literally, it's a "good word" to us from God, something many Christians are familiar with. It's a good way to end now, too: Go in God's peace.

Why a benediction, though? We've traveled some distance in these pages, as I've tried to share with you some of my thinking on personality disorders and problem people, on brain science and its fascinating intersection with faith, on tools and disciplines that might help us make more sense out of ourselves and re-animate our journeys, on relationship — that core need to know and to be known by God and others. I haven't solved your big problems, to be sure. You're still left to deal with that angry man who sits in the front pew each Sunday. You'll likely be getting that e-mail from the disgruntled staff member who thinks he knows how to run the organization better than you do. Or perhaps you're reading this and saying to yourself, "And yes, I'm still stuck with that pastor who's written a book about helping but can't seem to help me!" As I said, your many problems have not been magically solved.

When a worship service ends and we necessarily return to the frantic lives that we live, we go forth having encountered — I hope — something of God's vision for our lives, and something of God himself. And I pray the same for this book. My hope is that you've become more aware of the depth and breadth of God's grace for complex, messy human beings like you and me. My hope is that you're convinced now that it's more important to be found than fixed. My hope is that you see yourself as much in need of grace as those who cause you headaches every day.

To lead and lead well, you must necessarily come to the end of yourself (your false self!), and find that this is yet a beginning of a new life, a new kind of leadership, animated by God's abiding Spirit in you. Living from your core, where the Spirit dwells, you can relinquish the need to fix, to control, and to conquer, and drink in God's life, a life animated by peace, rest, wholeness, love, forgiveness, and surrender. It's the good life.

Go in God's peace.

Notes

Notes to the Introduction

1. You can find the interview here: "Learning for a Change," *Fast Company* at http://www.fastcompany.com/36819/learning-change.

2. Eugene Peterson, *Pastor: A Memoir* (San Francisco: HarperOne, 2011), p. 210.

Notes to Chapter 1

1. These statistics are reported from the Fuller Institute, George Barna, and Pastoral Care Inc. at http://pastoralcareinc.com/WhyPastoralCare/Statistics.php.

2. Charles DeGroat, "Expectation versus Reality among Male Graduates of Seminary: A Phenomenological Study" (Saarbrücken: VDM Verlag, 2008).

3. Dan B. Allender, *Leading with a Limp* (Colorado Springs: WaterBrook Press, 2008), pp. 14-15.

4. Charles Spurgeon, "Our Position and Purpose," from http://www.biblebb.com/files/spurgeon/3245.htm.

5. Frederick Buechner, *Telling Secrets* (San Francisco: HarperOne, 1992), p. 38.

6. Arbinger Institute, *Leadership and Self-Deception: Getting Out of the Box* (San Francisco: Berrett-Koehler, 2010), p. xi.

7. David Gebler, *The Three Power Values: How Commitment, Integrity, and Transparency Clear the Roadblocks to Performance* (San Francisco: Jossey-Bass, 2012).

8. To better trace the themes of your story and how they impact your present and future, I highly recommend Dan Allender, *To Be Told: God Invites You to Co-Author Your Future* (Colorado Springs: WaterBrook Press, 2006).

9. Curt Thompson, *Anatomy of the Soul: Surprising Connections between Neuroscience and Spiritual Practices That Can Transform Your Life and Relationships* (Carol Stream, Ill.: Salt River, 2010), p. 77.

10. For more on mindfulness and neuroscience, see Daniel Siegel, *The Developing Mind* (New York: Guilford Press, 2012).

11. Quoted in Colin E. Gunton, *The Promise of Trinitarian Theology* (New York: T&T Clark, 1997), p. 94.

12. This is a phrase borrowed from my colleague, Mike Goheen. See Craig Bartholomew and Michael Goheen, *The True Story of the Whole World* (Grand Rapids: Faith Alive, 2009).

13. Indeed, as Christians who study interpersonal neurobiology are discovering, God's restoration project extends to the repair of our brain's neural pathways.

14. See Thompson, *Anatomy of the Soul.*

15. Allender, *Leading with a Limp,* p 3.

16. Ronald Richardson, *Creating a Healthier Church* (Minneapolis: Augsburg, 1996), p. 43.

Notes to Chapter 2

1. Quoted in Brent Curtis and John Eldredge, *The Sacred Romance* (Nashville: Thomas Nelson, 1997), p. 23.

2. David Whyte, *The Heart Aroused: Poetry and the Preservation of the Soul in Corporate America* (New York: Doubleday, 1994), p. 27.

3. Richard Rohr, *Hidden Things: Scripture as Spirituality* (Cincinnati: St. Anthony Messenger Press, 2008), p. 39.

4. See Stanley Grenz, *The Social God and the Relational Self* (Louisville: Westminster John Knox Press, 2001).

5. See J. Richard Middleton, *The Liberating Image: The* Imago Dei *in Genesis 1* (Grand Rapids: Brazos Press, 2005).

6. I believe in both the Christian doctrines of original goodness and original sin. My sense, however, is that the way it is explained is better cast in the larger biblical story that begins with a good creation, and in the larger scientific story which shows how wonderfully complex we are.

7. James Finley, *Merton's Palace of Nowhere* (Notre Dame, Ind.: Ave Maria Press, 1978), p. 30.

8. Thomas Lewis, Fari Amini, and Richard Lannon, *A General Theory of Love* (New York: Vintage Books, 2000), p. 131.

9. Curt Thompson, *Anatomy of the Soul: Surprising Connections between Neuroscience and Spiritual Practices That Can Transform Your Life and Relationships* (Carol Stream, Ill.: Salt River, 2010), p. 110.

10. William Wordsworth, *Poems in Two Volumes,* vol. 2 (Hamburg, Germany: Tredetion, 2011), p. 69.

11. See Robert Bly, *A Little Book on the Human Shadow* (New York: HarperCollins, 1988).

12. David G. Benner, *The Gift of Being Yourself: The Sacred Call to Self-Discovery* (Downers Grove, Ill.: InterVarsity Press, 2004), p. 78.

13. Frederick Buechner, *Telling Secrets* (San Francisco: HarperOne, 1992), pp. 44-45.

14. W. H. Auden, *Collected Poems* (New York: Random House, 2007), p. 530.

15. Thomas Merton, *New Seeds of Contemplation* (New York: New Directions, 1962), pp. 34-35.

Notes to Chapter 3

1. American Psychiatric Association, *Diagnostic and Statistical Manual of Mental Disorders: DSM-IV-TR,* 4th ed., rev. text (Washington, D.C.: American Psychiatric Association, 2000), p. 686.

2. Len Sperry, *Handbook of Diagnosis and Treatment of the DSM-IV Personality Disorders* (New York: Brunner/Mazel, 1995).

3. Marshall Shelley, *Well-Intentioned Dragons: Ministering to Problem People in the Church* (Minneapolis: Bethany House, 1994), p. 34.

4. Criteria for Narcissistic Personality Disorder can be found at http://www .mental-health-today.com/narcissistic/dsm.htm.

5. James F. Masterson, *The Search for the Real Self: Unmasking the Personality Disorders of Our Age* (New York: Free Press, 1990), p. 90.

6. See Chapter 2.

7. Frederick Buechner, *Telling Secrets* (San Francisco: HarperOne, 1992), p. 56.

8. "Discipline" is always about "discipleship," using even the means of tough love to bring someone back to a place of wholeness and into the community.

9. American Psychological Association, *Diagnostic and Statistical Manual of Mental Disorders,* 4th ed. (Washington, D.C.: American Psychological Association, 1994), p. 710. Criteria for Borderline Personality Disorder can be found online at http://www .borderlinepersonalitytoday.com/main/dsmiv.htm.

10. Do not mistake OCPD for a somewhat similar mood disorder, which is commonly associated with behaviors like chronic hand-washing. Criteria for Obsessive-Compulsive Personality Disorder can be found at http://psychcentral.com/disorders/ sx26.htm.

11. I've recommended *Good Will Hunting* starring Matt Damon, *The Kid* starring Bruce Willis, and *Life as a House* starring Kevin Kline. Each seems to get beneath the surface in its own way.

12. Criteria for Histrionic Personality Disorder can be found at http://www.ncbi .nlm.nih.gov/pubmedhealth/PMH0002498/.

13. Andrew Purves, *The Crucifixion of Ministry: Surrendering Our Ambitions to the Service of Christ* (Downers Grove, Ill.: InterVarsity Press, 2007), p. 21.

14. This wisdom comes from Johnny LaLonde, a colleague at City Church San Francisco Counseling Center.

Notes to Chapter 4

1. Gerald G. May, *Addiction and Grace: Love and Spirituality in the Healing of Addictions* (New York: HarperCollins, 1988), p. 11.

2. See my book *Leaving Egypt: Finding God in the Wilderness Places* (Grand Rapids: Faith Alive, 2011). This is, in some respects, an entire book on the topic of addiction.

3. Bill Plotkin, *Soulcraft: Crossing into the Mysteries of Nature and Psyche* (New World Library, Kindle edition, 2008), p. 90.

4. Bob Goudzwaard, David Van Heemst, and Mark Vander Vennen, *Hope in Troubled Times* (Grand Rapids: Baker Academic, 2007), p. 43.

5. May, *Addiction and Grace*, p. 14.

6. William Cope Moyers, *Broken: My Story of Addiction and Redemption* (New York: Viking/Penguin, 2006).

7. Robert E. Quinn, *Deep Change: Discovering the Leader Within,* Jossey-Bass Business & Management Series (San Francisco: Jossey-Bass, 1996), p. 11.

8. Though I've made some changes, for this basic framework I am deeply indebted to F. LeRon Shults and Steven J. Sandage, *Transforming Spirituality: Integrating Theology and Psychology* (Grand Rapids: Baker Academic, 2006).

9. See Eric Johnson, *Foundations of Soul Care* (Downers Grove, Ill.: InterVarsity Press, 2007), p. 586.

10. Because we cannot cover every addiction or every contingency, refer to the Resources appendix at the back of the book, and consult with a local specialist.

11. Sharon Hersh, *The Last Addiction: Own Your Desire, Live beyond Recovery, Find Lasting Freedom* (Colorado Springs: WaterBrook Press, 2008).

12. Thomas Keating, *The Human Condition: Contemplation and Transformation* (New York: Paulist Press, 1999), p. 38.

Notes to Chapter 5

1. Dan B. Allender and Tremper Longman III, *Bold Love* (Colorado Springs: NavPress, 1992). I've been teaching Dan and Tremper's material for nearly fifteen years. Though I articulate things in my own way, I cannot express how indebted I am to their insights.

2. M. Craig Barnes, *The Pastor as Minor Poet: Texts and Subtexts in the Ministerial Life* (Grand Rapids: Wm. B. Eerdmans, 2009), p. 16.

3. Allender and Longman, *Bold Love*, p. 255.

4. Frederick Buechner, *Telling Secrets* (San Francisco: HarperOne, 1992), p. 44.

5. See my blog entry of May 25, 2009: "Does being like Jesus mean staying with an abuser?" at http://bit.ly/h298Yc.

6. See Sid Rosen, *My Voice Will Go with You: The Teaching Tales of Milton H. Erickson* (New York: W. W. Norton, 1991).

7. Allender and Longman, *Bold Love,* p. 19.

8. George Victor, *Hitler: The Pathology of Evil* (Dulles, Va.: Brassey's, 1998), p. 30.

9. For more on the diagnosis of a sociopath, see http://www.ncbi.nlm.nih.gov/pubmedhealth/PMH0001919/.

10. I recommend books about dealing with abusers in the Resource section at the end of this book.

11. On the fear of God as relinquishing control, see Choon-Leong Seow, *Ecclesiastes,* Anchor Bible Commentary (New Haven: Yale University Press, 1997), p. 50.

Notes to Chapter 6

1. Jerry Sittser, *A Grace Disguised: How the Soul Grows through Loss* (Grand Rapids: Zondervan, 2004), p. 47.

2. Iain Matthew, *The Impact of God: Soundings from St. John of the Cross* (London: Hodder & Stoughton, 1995), p. 10.

3. Matthew, *The Impact of God,* p. 60.

4. John Flavel, *A Saint Indeed; Or, The Great Work of a Christian in Keeping the Heart in the Several Conditions of Life,* available at http://www.ccel.org/ccel/flavel/saintindeed.txt.

5. Matthew, *The Impact of God,* p. 15.

6. F. LeRon Shults and Steven J. Sandage, *Transforming Spirituality: Integrating Theology and Psychology* (Grand Rapids: Baker Academic, 2006), p. 27.

7. St. John of the Cross, *The Dark Night of the Soul* (New York: Evergreen Review Inc., 2009), Book 1 5.3.

8. Daniel P. Schrock, *The Dark Night: A Gift of God* (Harrisonburg, Va.: Herald Press, 2009), p. 27.

9. Thomas Merton, *New Seeds of Contemplation* (New York: New Directions, 1961), p. 34.

10. Robert E. Quinn, *Deep Change: Discovering the Leader Within,* Jossey-Bass Business & Management Series (San Francisco: Jossey-Bass, 1996), p. 45.

11. Sittser, *A Grace Disguised,* p. 63.

12. Richard Rohr, *Falling Upwards: A Spirituality for the Two Halves of Life* (San Francisco: Jossey-Bass, 2011), p. xxiii.

13. Schrock, *The Dark Night,* p. 58.

14. Miroslav Volf, *Exclusion and Embrace: A Theological Exploration of Identity, Otherness, and Reconciliation* (Nashville: Abingdon Press, 1996), p. 294.

15. Susan Howatch, *Glittering Images* (New York: Fawcett, 1988), p. 224.

Notes to Chapter 7

1. Søren Kierkegaard, *Purity of Heart Is to Will One Thing* (San Francisco: Harper, 2011).

2. Charles Spurgeon, "A Divided Heart," Sept. 25, 1859; find this at http://www.biblebb.com/files/spurgeon/0276.htm.

3. Parker Palmer, *A Hidden Wholeness: The Journey toward an Undivided Life* (San Francisco: Jossey-Bass, 2004), p. 34.

4. David Whyte, in an excerpt from "Crossing the Unknown Sea," at http://www.gratefulness.org/readings/whyte_dsr.htm.

5. Jacob Neusner, *Theology of the Halakah*, at http://www.scribd.com/doc/61265049/Theology-of-the-Halakhah-Jacob-Neusner.

6. David Whyte, *The Heart Aroused: Poetry and the Preservation of the Soul in Corporate America* (New York: Doubleday, 1994), p. 7.

7. Palmer, *A Hidden Wholeness*, p. 5.

8. Palmer, *A Hidden Wholeness*, p. 4.

9. Richard Rohr, *Breathing under Water: Spirituality and the Twelve Steps* (Cincinnati: St. Anthony Messenger Press, 2011), p. 9.

10. See my book *Leaving Egypt: Finding God in the Wilderness Places* (Grand Rapids: Faith Alive, 2011), where I explore this biblical pattern of transformation through the biblical story of the Exodus from Egypt.

11. See Chapter 4 in Richard Rohr's *Breathing under Water*.

12. See David G. Benner, *Care of Souls: Revisioning Christian Nurture and Counsel* (Grand Rapids: Baker, 1998).

13. Parker, *A Hidden Wholeness*, p. 20.

14. David G. Benner, *Spirituality and the Awakening Self: The Sacred Journey of Transformation* (Grand Rapids: Brazos Press, 2012), p. 60.

15. Benner, *Spirituality and the Awakening Self*, p. 33.

Notes to Chapter 8

1. Robert E. Quinn, *Deep Change: Discovering the Leader Within*, Jossey-Bass Business & Management Series (San Francisco: Jossey-Bass, 1996), p. 11.

2. Marshall Goldsmith, *Mojo* (New York: Hyperion, 2009), p. 93.

3. Wesley Granberg-Michaelson, *Leadership from the Inside Out: Spirituality and Organizational Change* (New York: Crossway, 2004), p. 13.

4. Richard Rohr, *Breathing under Water: Spirituality and the Twelve Steps* (Cincinnati: St. Anthony Messenger Press, 2011), p. 33.

5. Curt Thompson, *Anatomy of the Soul: Surprising Connections between Neuroscience*

and Spiritual Practices That Can Transform Your Life and Relationships (Carol Stream, Ill.: Salt River, 2010), p. 3.

6. Thompson, *Anatomy of the Soul*, p. 23.

7. Parker Palmer, *A Hidden Wholeness: The Journey toward an Undivided Life* (San Francisco: Jossey-Bass, 2004), p. 39.

8. Quinn, *Deep Change*, p. 11.

9. Henri Nouwen, *Making All Things New* (New York: Harper, 1981), p. 70.

10. From the introduction to Teresa of Ávila's *The Interior Castle*, trans. Mirabai Starr (New York: Riverhead Books, 2003).

11. Richard Bauckham makes this point wonderfully and frequently in his *Theology of the Book of Revelation* (Cambridge: Cambridge University Press, 1993).

12. A site for the Daily Office I use is http://www.missionstclare.com/english/index .html. See also *Seeking God's Face*, Faith Alive Christian Resources.

13. A site for the Daily Examen I use is http://www.sacredspace.ie/.

14. For more on the labyrinth, see http://www.gracecathedral.org/visit/labyrinth/.

15. For more on this, see the chapter "The Unbusy Pastor" in Eugene Peterson, *The Contemplative Pastor* (Grand Rapids: Wm. B. Eerdmans, 1989).

16. For more on the significance of intentional practices and the cultural habits which form us, see James K. A. Smith, *Desiring the Kingdom: Worship, Worldview, and Cultural Formation* (Grand Rapids: Baker Academic, 2009).

Resources

ABUSE (SEXUAL)

Dan B. Allender. *The Wounded Heart: Hope for Adult Victims of Childhood Sexual Abuse*. Rev. ed. Colorado Springs: NavPress, 1995.

Justin and Lindsey Holcomb. *Rid of My Disgrace: Hope and Healing for Victims of Sexual Assault*. Wheaton, Ill.: Crossway, 2011.

Diane Mandt Langberg. *On the Threshold of Hope*. Wheaton, Ill.: Tyndale House, 1999.

ABUSE (EMOTIONAL/PSYCHOLOGICAL)

Lundy Bancroft. *Why Does He Do That? Inside the Minds of Angry and Controlling Men*. New York: Berkley Books, 2003.

Patricia Evans. *The Verbally Abusive Relationship: How to Recognize It and How to Respond*. Avon, Mass.: Adams Media, 2003.

Gregory L. Jantz (with Ann McMurray). *Healing the Scars of Emotional Abuse*. Grand Rapids: Baker, 1995.

ABUSE (DOMESTIC)

Helen L. Conway. *Domestic Violence and the Church*. Milton Keynes, U.K.: Paternoster Press, 1998.

Justin and Lindsey Holcomb. *Is It My Fault? Hope and Healing for Those Suffering Domestic Violence*. Chicago: Moody Publishers, 2014.

Neil Jacobson and John Gottman. *When Men Batter Women: New Insights into Ending Abusive Relationships*. New York: Simon & Schuster, 1998.

Addictions (General)

Sharon Hersh. *The Last Addiction: Own Your Desire, Live beyond Recovery, Find Lasting Freedom.* Colorado Springs: WaterBrook Press, 2008.

Gerald G. May. *Addiction and Grace: Love and Spirituality in the Healing of Addictions.* New York: HarperCollins, 1988.

Addictions (Sexual)

Claudia Black. *Deceived: Facing Sexual Betrayal, Lies, and Secrets.* Center City, Minn.: Hazelden, 2009.

Patrick Carnes. *Facing the Shadow: Starting Sexual and Relationship Recovery* (Workbook). Wickenburg, Ariz.: Gentle Path, 2001.

Patrick Carnes. *Out of the Shadows: Understanding Sexual Addiction.* 3rd ed. Center City, Minn.: Hazelden, 2001.

Patrick Carnes, David L. Delmonico, and Elizabeth Griffin, with Joseph M. Moriarty. *In the Shadows of the Net: Breaking Free of Compulsive Online Sexual Behavior.* Center City, Minn.: Hazelden, 2007.

Patrick Carnes, with Joseph M. Moriarty. *Sexual Anorexia: Overcoming Sexual Self-Hatred.* Center City, Minn.: Hazelden, 1997.

Stephanie Carnes. *Mending the Shattered Heart: A Guide for Partners of Sex Addicts.* 2nd ed. Carefree, Ariz.: Gentle Path Press, 2011.

Michael John Cusick. *Surfing for God: Discovering the Divine Desire beneath Sexual Struggle.* Nashville: Thomas Nelson, 2012.

Marnie C. Ferree. *No Stones: Women Redeemed from Sexual Addiction.* 2nd ed. Downers Grove, Ill.: InterVarsity Press, 2010.

Debra Laaser. *Shattered Vows: Hope and Healing for Women Who Have Been Sexually Betrayed.* Grand Rapids: Zondervan, 2008.

Mark R. Laaser. *Healing the Wounds of Sexual Addiction.* Grand Rapids: Zondervan, 2004.

Addictions (Substance)

Caroline Knapp. *Drinking: A Love Story.* New York: Dial Press, 1997.

Michael J. Kuhar. *The Addicted Brain: Why We Abuse Drugs, Alcohol, and Nicotine.* Upper Saddle River, N.J.: FT Press, 2012.

William Cope Moyers. *Broken: My Story of Addiction and Redemption.* New York: Viking/Penguin, 2006.

Addictions (Other)

Margaret Bullitt-Jonas. *A Holy Hunger: A Memoir of Desire.* New York: Alfred A. Knopf, 1999.

Steven Levenkron. *Cutting: Understanding and Overcoming Self-Mutilation.* New York: W. W. Norton, 2006.

Michele Siegel, Judith Brisman, and Margot Weinshel. *Surviving an Eating Disorder: Strategies for Families and Friends.* 3rd ed. New York: Collins Living, 1999.

Attachment Relationships

Tim Clinton and Gary Sibcy. *Attachments: Why You Love, Feel, and Act the Way You Do.* Brentwood, Tenn.: Integrity Publishers, 2002.

Robert Karen. *Becoming Attached: First Relationships and How They Shape Our Capacity to Love.* New York: Oxford University Press, 1994.

Church and Counseling

Julie A. Gorman. *Community That Is Christian.* 2nd ed. Grand Rapids: Baker, 2002.

Theresa F. Latini. *The Church and the Crisis of Community: A Practical Theology of Small-Group Ministry.* Grand Rapids: Wm. B. Eerdmans, 2011.

Ronald Richardson. *Creating a Healthier Church*. Minneapolis: Augsburg, 1996.

Rod Wilson. *Counseling and Community*. Dallas: Word, 1995.

COUNSELING SKILLS

Deborah van Deusen Hunsinger and Theresa F. Latini. *Transforming Church Conflict: Compassionate Leadership in Action*. Louisville: Westminster John Knox Press, 2013.

Scott T. Meier and Susan R. Davis. *The Elements of Counseling*. 7th ed. Belmont, Calif.: Wadsworth Cengage Learning, 2011.

DIVORCE AND REMARRIAGE

David Instone-Brewer. *Divorce and Remarriage in the Bible: Biblical Solutions for Pastoral Realities*. Downers Grove, Ill.: InterVarsity Press, 2003.

David Instone-Brewer. *Divorce and Remarriage in the Bible: The Social and Literary Context*. Grand Rapids: Wm. B. Eerdmans, 2002.

EMOTIONS

Dan B. Allender and Tremper Longman III. *The Cry of the Soul: How Our Emotions Reveal Our Deepest Questions about God*. Colorado Springs: NavPress, 1994.

Matthew Elliot. *Feel: The Power of Listening to Your Heart*. Wheaton, Ill.: Tyndale House, 2008.

ENNEAGRAM

The Enneagram is a personality assessment tool with a unique connection to the seven deadly sins in the Christian tradition, and wisdom from the Christian contemplative tradition on soul care.

Beatrice Chestnut. *The Complete Enneagram: 27 Paths to Greater Self-Knowledge.* Berkeley, Calif.: She Writes Press, 2013.

David N. Daniels and Virginia A. Price. *The Essential Enneagram: The Definitive Personality Test and Self-Discovery Guide.* Rev. ed. New York: HarperOne, 2009.

Simon Parke. *The Enneagram: A Private Conversation with the World's Greatest Psychologist.* Oxford: Lion, 2008.

Don Richard Riso and Russ Hudson. *The Wisdom of the Enneagram: The Complete Guide to Psychological and Spiritual Growth for the Nine Personality Types.* New York: Bantam Books, 1999.

Richard Rohr and Andreas Ebert. *The Enneagram: A Christian Perspective.* New York: Crossroad, 2001.

ETHICS

Richard M. Gula. *Just Ministry: Professional Ethics for Pastoral Ministers.* New York: Paulist Press, 2010.

FAILURE AND IMPERFECTION

Dan B. Allender. *Leading with a Limp.* Colorado Springs: WaterBrook Press, 2008.

Brené Brown. *The Gifts of Imperfection: Let Go of Who You Think You're Supposed to Be and Embrace Who You Are.* Center City, Minn.: Hazelden, 2010.

Ernest Kurtz and Katherine Ketcham. *The Spirituality of Imperfection: Modern Wisdom from Classic Stories.* New York: Bantam Books, 1992. 2008.

LOSS, GRIEF, AND DISAPPOINTMENT

Renée Altson. *Stumbling toward Faith: My Longing to Heal from the Evil that God Allowed.* Grand Rapids: Zondervan, 2004.

Larry Crabb. *Shattered Dreams: God's Unexpected Path to Joy.* Colorado Springs: WaterBrook Press, 2001.

C. S. Lewis. *A Grief Observed.* San Francisco: HarperSanFrancisco, 2001.

St. John of the Cross. *The Dark Night of the Soul.*

Jerry Sittser. *A Grace Disguised: How the Soul Grows through Loss.* Grand Rapids: Zondervan, 2004.

Nicholas Wolterstorff. *Lament for a Son.* Grand Rapids: Wm. B. Eerdmans, 1987.

MARRIAGE

Dan B. Allender and Tremper Longman III. *Intimate Allies.* Wheaton, Ill.: Tyndale House, 1995.

John M. Gottman, Julie Schwartz Gottman, and Joan DeClaire. *Ten Lessons to Transform Your Marriage.* New York: Crown Publishers, 2006.

Archibald D. Hart and Sharon Hart Morris. *Safe Haven Marriage: A Marriage You Can Come Home To.* Nashville: W Publishing Group, 2003.

Mike Mason. *The Mystery of Marriage: Meditations on the Miracle.* Sisters, Ore.: Multnomah Books, 1996.

NEUROSCIENCE

David Brooks. *The Social Animal: The Hidden Sources of Love, Character, and Achievement.* New York: Random House, 2012.

Thomas Lewis, Fari Amini, and Richard Lannon. *A General Theory of Love.* New York: Vintage Books, 2000.

Curt Thompson. *Anatomy of the Soul: Surprising Connections between Neuroscience and Spiritual Practices That Can Transform Your Life and Relationships.* Carol Stream, Ill.: Salt River, 2010.

PARENTING

Dan B. Allender. *How Children Raise Parents: The Art of Listening to Your Family.* Colorado Springs: WaterBrook Press, 2003.

Foster W. Cline and Jim Fay. *Parenting with Love and Logic: Teaching Children Responsibility.* Updated and expanded ed. Colorado Springs: Piñon Press, 2006.

PASTORAL CHARACTER

M. Craig Barnes. *The Pastor as Minor Poet: Texts and Subtexts in the Ministerial Life.* Grand Rapids: Wm. B. Eerdmans, 2009.

Eugene H. Peterson. *The Contemplative Pastor: Returning to the Art of Spiritual Direction.* Grand Rapids: Wm. B. Eerdmans, 1989.

Eugene H. Peterson. *Under the Unpredictable Plant: An Exploration in Vocational Holiness.* Grand Rapids: Wm. B. Eerdmans, 1992.

PERSONALITY DISORDERS

Lorna Smith Benjamin. *Interpersonal Diagnosis and Treatment of Personality Disorders.* New York: Guilford Press, 1993.

Jeffrey J. Magnavita. *Relational Therapy for Personality Disorders.* New York: Wiley, 2000.

James F. Masterson. *Search for the Real Self: Unmasking the Personality Disorders of Our Age.* New York: Free Press, 1990.

RELATIONAL INTEGRITY

Dan B. Allender and Tremper Longman III. *Bold Love.* Colorado Springs: NavPress, 1992.

Parker Palmer. *A Hidden Wholeness: The Journey toward an Undivided Life.* San Francisco: Jossey-Bass, 2004.

Ronald W. Richardson. *Becoming a Healthier Pastor: Family Systems Theory and the Pastor's Own Family.* Minneapolis: Fortress Press, 2005.

Soul Care in Christian History

David G. Benner. *Care of Souls: Revisioning Christian Nurture and Counsel.* Grand Rapids: Baker, 1998.

Eric Johnson. *Foundations of Soul Care.* Downers Grove, Ill.: Inter-Varsity Press, 2007.

Spiritual Disciplines

The Daily Office: http://www.missionstclare.com/english/.

Gerald G. May. *The Awakened Heart: Living beyond Addiction.* San Francisco: HarperSanFrancisco, 1991.

Henri J. M. Nouwen. *With Open Hands.* 2nd rev. ed. Notre Dame, Ind.: Ave Maria Press, 2006.

Philip F. Reinders. *Seeking God's Face: Praying with the Bible through the Year.* Grand Rapids: Faith Alive Christian Resources, 2010.

Daniel Wolpert. *Creating a Life with God: The Call of Ancient Prayer Practices.* Nashville: Upper Room Books, 2003.

Spiritual Maturity and Transformation

Chuck DeGroat. *Leaving Egypt: Finding God in the Wilderness Places.* Grand Rapids: Faith Alive, 2011.

Iain Matthew. *The Impact of God: Soundings from St. John of the Cross.* London: Hodder & Stoughton, 1995.

Richard Rohr. *Falling Upwards: A Spirituality for the Two Halves of Life.* San Francisco: Jossey-Bass, 2011.

F. LeRon Shults and Steven J. Sandage. *Transforming Spirituality: Integrating Theology and Psychology.* Grand Rapids: Baker Academic, 2006.

STORY

Dan Allender. *To Be Told: God Invites You to Co-Author Your Future.* Colorado Springs: WaterBrook Press, 2006.

Frederick Buechner. *Telling Secrets.* San Francisco: HarperOne, 1992.

Brent Curtis and John Eldredge. *The Sacred Romance.* Nashville: Thomas Nelson, 1997.

George MacDonald. *The Diary of an Old Soul: 366 Writings for Devotional Reflection.* Minneapolis: Augsburg, 1965.

TRUE SELF AND UNION WITH GOD

David G. Benner. *The Gift of Being Yourself: The Sacred Call to Self-Discovery.* Downers Grove, Ill.: InterVarsity Press, 2004.

James Finley. *Merton's Palace of Nowhere.* Notre Dame, Ind.: Ave Maria Press, 1978.

James Martin, S.J. *Becoming Who You Are: Insights on the True Self from Thomas Merton and Other Saints.* Mahwah, N.J.: Hidden-Spring, 2006.

Thomas Merton. *New Seeds of Contemplation.* New York: New Directions, 1962.

Henri J. M. Nouwen. *Return of the Prodigal Son: A Story of Homecoming.* New York: Continuum, 1995.

Richard Rohr. *Immortal Diamond: The Search for Our True Self.* San Francisco: Jossey-Bass, 2013.

VOCATION

Os Guinness. *The Call: Finding and Fulfilling the Central Purpose of Your Life.* Nashville: W Pub. Group, 2003.

John Neafsey. *A Sacred Voice Is Calling: Personal Vocation and Social Conscience.* Maryknoll, N.Y.: Orbis Books, 2006.

Parker J. Palmer. *Let Your Life Speak: Listening for the Voice of Vocation.* San Francisco: Jossey-Bass, 2000.